THE
ENTREPRENEUR'S
FACES

HOW MAKERS, VISIONARIES AND
OUTSIDERS SUCCEED

JONATHAN LITTMAN
SUSANNA CAMP

SNOWBALL
NARRATIVE
PRESS

Sausalito, California

Library of Congress Control Number: 2020904540
Library of Congress-in-Publication Data:
Names: Littman, Jonathan, author. | Camp, Susanna, author.
Title: The Entrepreneur's Faces: How Makers, Visionaries and Outsiders Succeed
Description: First Edition | California: Snowball Narrative, 2020
Subjects: Business | Entrepreneurship

ISBN 978-1-7347233-2-8
eBook ISBN 978-1-7347233-1-1

Printed in the United States of America

Cover design by Max James
Interior layout and typesetting by Ahmed El Bayoumi
Visit our website at www.theentrepreneursfaces.com

Praise for *The Entrepreneur's Faces*

"There's only one Steve Jobs but Littman and Camp show there are many paths to becoming a successful entrepreneur. This engaging, accessible book demystifies the essential process that they all go through – and that you can too."
– Peter Leyden, Founder of Reinvent and Host of the What's Now: San Francisco event series

"The beautiful and insightful descriptions of the different types of entrepreneurs and the clear explanation of the phases a company passes through, have given me new insights that are very useful in the conversations I have with local entrepreneurs about further strengthening the ecosystem. A must read for government leaders who want to understand how successful entrepreneurs think and act."
– Bas Beekman, Director, Startup Amsterdam

"Littman and Camp spin real-life stories that read like thrillers, keeping you turning the page to find out what happens next. Read *The Entrepreneur's Faces* as a guide and companion to remind you that you are not alone in your struggles on the often tumultuous but ultimately rewarding journey of being an entrepreneur. Enjoy!"
– John S. Couch, Author of *The Art of Creative Rebellion* and VP of Product Design, Hulu

"Through deeply personal storytelling, Littman and Camp have identified the traits and characteristics that form the essential DNA of an entrepreneur. In doing so, readers will recognize these elements in themselves and ultimately create their own recipe for success to help them along their journey. Required reading for anyone ever considering starting their own business."
– Phil Kearney, Chief Operating Officer, Vertical Mass, Managing Partner Southgate Advisors

"There is no finer introduction to the world of the entrepreneur. Rather than looking at this universe as some sort of unicorn zoo, Littman and Camp deconstruct their subjects into specific types and present their journeys in an accessible fashion that is a true guidebook to being an entrepreneur."
– Harvey Myman, Partner, Element 8 Entertainment

"*The Entrepreneur's Faces* clearly shows us that entrepreneurship – far from being a linear trajectory – is a diverse journey filled with significant ups and downs, and that there are different paths to success and different types of entrepreneurs. This timely book defines a powerful typology of entrepreneurship that is helpful for those thinking about embarking on this journey, and for those of us who support or invest in those taking the great leap. A must-read!"
– Nuno Gonçalves Pedro, Founder and Managing Partner, Strive Capital

"*The Entrepreneur's Faces* goes to the heart of entrepreneurship, capturing the personal journeys of ten founders and their struggle and passion to succeed. Beautifully written, these stories illustrate the seven essential stages on the hero's journey of building a successful company."
– Steve Hoffman, CEO of Founders Space, Author of *Make Elephants Fly*

Praise for *The Art of Innovation* & *The Ten Faces of Innovation*

"Jonathan Littman, my coauthor, not only shouldered most of the heavy lifting during creation of the first manuscript, but also taught me a lot about writing in the process. I gained new respect for his profession and am anxious to see his future works."
– Tom Kelley, *The Art of Innovation*

"On nearly every page, the story of some upstart invention is recounted in patter that's as good as a skilled magician's…Almost like visiting an IDEO Workshop in person."
– Cory Doctorow, *Wired*

"Essential reading for every single person in your organization – even the CEO should read it! Each page contains a nugget that's worth the price of the entire book. Wow."
– Seth Godin, Author of *Purple Cow* and *Tribe*

THE
ENTREPRENEUR'S
FACES

INTRODUCTION

What sparks your curiosity, fuels your passions, and provides that extra jolt of motivation? We believe the answer lies within, in a novel, deeper understanding of that sometimes elusive persona – yourself. And yet, there's a paradox. Even as you come to know and trust your core identity, you also embrace the importance of transformation, learning to shift who you are, and how you approach obstacles and opportunities. In the world of startups and entrepreneurship, we're all constantly reminded of how we must be *agile* and adept at *fast prototyping*. We must fail fast, and of course, *pivot*. These are all perfectly valid skills and capabilities. While there are excellent, robust systems out there such as Lean Startup and Business Model Canvas, they are focused on product development or startups themselves. To fully embrace this new proactive way of being requires an essential reboot in your approach to life and work. Pinpointing who you are and what other types of people speak to you or your challenges is foundational. It's about finding both a personal compass and the wind to fill your sails.

And then came the Black Swan of the pandemic. Does that crisis – or others like it – make the entrepreneurial mindset obsolete? Far from it. History proves that recessions, downturns, and yes, pandemics, demand that we respond to the threat with tremendous creativity and innovation. Business as usual no longer exists. Companies that can't shake off their standard operational dogma will struggle. The same applies to people. Many will end up paralyzed like deer in the headlights. In contrast, the resilience gained from failing forward might just help you survive real-world Darwinian scenarios.

Our book began with the idea of creating a fresh, human centered model for transformation. We didn't see the value in building another Myers-Briggs or DiSC Assessment, diagnostic tests that assign a one-dimensional profile. Nor did we want to construct some new master organizational model, pen another hagiography of a legendary entrepreneur, or create some new magical "follow these steps and out comes your innovation" formula. Instead, we asked a simple question: What if you could tap the power of the most accomplished innovators, entrepreneurs and founders in the world? If you knew how they each forged a winning template for success, could you surface that power in yourself?

We're human, and to truly shift behaviors can be hard. Cultivating a mindset of innovation, creativity and entrepreneurship is an intensely personal quest, and there's no better guidance on this arduous path than a direct window into the lives of real people starting on this same journey of exploration and growth. *The Entrepreneur's Faces* will help you identify the ten essential entrepreneurial types to propel your professional growth, and better gauge potential partners on the journey. The ten individuals profiled in the book are each characterized by an emblematic type, people who master challenges with a characteristic approach, and echo the models and behaviors of renowned innovators and entrepreneurs. They're archetypes, or Faces, and we know from our workshops that you'll be drawn to find yourself in a few of these Faces, to identify with our protagonists' strengths, in their profiles, stories, and enduring lessons.

These are real, approachable entrepreneurs, windows into the furious drive and passion transforming business today. Our heroes symbolize a revolutionary movement in how people today take charge of their lives and careers, in how you too can take proactive steps. One after another, our characters find a spark in a pain or friction – the ache of middle age that hatches a radical idea to free us from the stifling office chair, a terribly shy young engineer who discovers a latent gift for helping corporate competitors collaborate. You will see yourself in the successes and struggles of these seemingly everyday people who all embraced a conscious decision to become extraordinary. They range from young to middle age, drawn from all walks of life. In these pages, you'll encounter a concert pianist, a physicist, a veteran of Y Combinator, a Stanford Law student and many more – an eclectic collection of inspired individuals whose stories will grab you. Just as our brains create fresh neural pathways when we engage in new activities and mental stimulation we see these ten entrepreneurial "pathways" as a powerful way to open yourself to new possibilities for self-growth, to virtually step into the shoes of others who have climbed the mountain.

The Entrepreneur's Faces is about personal journeys, change and transformation. Our characters set out on divergent paths. They must overcome pain and setbacks, leap boundaries and demonstrate tremendous vision, imagination and drive. They don't all end up at the same place, but they do pass through the same seven essential stages, points on this hero's journey for an entrepreneur. We call this process The Arc.

While the Faces help you determine who you are, and the distinct nature of your entrepreneurial mindset, The Arc provides a roadmap to get you where you want to go. These are the tangible steps in the process. Think about accelerating your project, product or career in a 3-D fashion. The core phases are essential for entrepreneurial change. It's great to know who you aspire to be. But it's in the seven stages of The Arc where you find out how far you're ready to go:

The Awakening – Tap curiosity and a discovery mindset for new possibilities.

The Shift – Embrace the unknown, break from anchors, take tangible steps.

The Place – Connect with the people, community, and place where you thrive.

The Launch – Deep-dive into prototyping, and get your venture moving.

The Money – Secure the cash and backing to get real.

The Test – Iterate, iterate, iterate. Run the gauntlet of prototyping and troubleshooting. It's do-or-die time.

The Scale – Expand potential through technology, delegation, and partnership. Climb the last peak.

The Arc illuminates the entrepreneurial process in a holistic, straightforward framework we think you will find invaluable as you dive into starting your company or pursuing your next venture. And there's another factor that we firmly believe infuses our characters' trials with meaning. We view them as a cohort or class of entrepreneurs. They are all on the same basic trajectory, and as you read their stories we invite you to think about what each of them might have learned from one another. How the unique approach and perspective of a different face might have afforded them a competitive edge.

In many ways our ten characters and our narrative is a microcosm of this global phenomenon. In November of 2017 when we began the research for this book, during an extended tour of Europe, we couldn't possibly know or anticipate the full trajectory of their journeys. Nothing was planned, nothing was fixed, including who would end up profiled in our book. We consider ourselves fortunate to have found these engaging and distinctly individual founders mid-flight, and think that the unpredictability and variety of their experience reinforces many essential elements of entrepreneurism.

We invite you to join them on this expedition.

1 —The Awakening—

He wasn't even sure what it meant to be an entrepreneur. What he did know was that he didn't want to have to go and ask permission.

Welcome to the Awakening, the crucial first step on the path to growth, where we fundamentally shift how we see the world, professionally and personally. We call this adopting a mindset of discovery, a new paradigm that brings an intense curiosity about ourselves, ideas, and how things are made or sold.

The Awakening is about character too. It's about who you are becoming as much as what you hope to do. We think of the Awakening as foundational, the essential grounding and support necessary for launching this formative journey. Because there will be countless times when you will doubt yourself, when you will wonder, *Why can't I just do something normal, like everyone else?*

It's easy to be lulled into complacency. You may already have a job, enjoy the security of a steady income, or be tracked into a certain, promising career path. The Awakening blows in a newfound sense of openness. It may start with reading a great book, discovering an inspiring TED Talk, or getting dragged to a meetup. What's different is that these experiences jolt you into thinking there's something more.

Everyone's Awakening is unique, and our core characters provide us with telling real-world examples of how specific Faces – say, the Maker, the Visionary or the Athlete – shape how you awaken. This is how it happened for the character we call the Leader. Adrift as a young man, he happened upon a lecture that triggered his innate courage and imagination, and would ultimately inspire him to alter the course of his life. The change in behavior during the Awakening can be just that spontaneous and stark. Quite suddenly you're open to grabbing a coffee with people outside your core group, attending unusual events, and that's where you expand your potential. Here's what may not seem obvious at first glance. With just a few changes in where you go and who you connect with, you multiply the chances that you will find that missing purpose, that galvanizing idea, or ideal collaborator you've long been seeking.

The Awakening is about inquisitiveness, about cataloging and curating, trying to make sense of a new field. You aren't always sure why you're pursuing this new interest, but in the process something big happens: you become a trend-spotter, a database builder, and yes, an expert. The Accidental had his Awakening in just such a way. He started tapping supercomputers and writing AI code for his personal goal of learning French, never anticipating it would amount to anything more than a hobby.

The Awakening is about something unseen. A surging rush of confidence. You begin to believe you're capable of more than you'd planned. More than others had expected. You begin to trust that the process is worthwhile and rewarding in and of itself. You become less concerned about what you will discover, and more confident that each day you are growing stronger and more capable, more prepared to capitalize on whatever is next.

Pain too can spark an Awakening. Getting fired. Being overlooked for a promotion, stymied in your job, or simply waking up one morning, and seeing no viable runway to advance in your career. Everyone feels these pains, but if this is your Awakening, you don't whine, become depressed, or scale back your dream. It doesn't matter why you failed. Maybe you were in the wrong place and time? Maybe office politics conspired against you? Whatever the reason, failing frees you from your set path, and provides a sudden, sharp awareness that you were on the wrong track, and that there may be another far more interesting game.

This may sound counter-intuitive, but success can also deliver a pain that helps you to awaken. You become very good at what you do. You do it well for years or decades and wake up one day with this odd epiphany: *Success is holding me back. All the money, recognition, and comfort I'm finding in a risk-free career ... is not enough.*

The awakened takes stock of his or her surroundings and thinks, *This doesn't work ...* or, *This could be so much better!* What sets them apart is that they have the patience to stay with that pain. They name it. Feel it. They examine the problem from all kinds of angles. This is, after all, the Awakening. It's when you slow down long enough to consider another path.

The Maker
Perry Klebahn
Stanford University

The Maker, the prototypical entrepreneur, brings a tireless, feverish commitment: stubborn, single-minded, obsessed. Makers prototype like mad and view mistakes as fast feedback, the best and quickest way to focus their product and bring it to a paying customer. Unfazed by obstacles, the Maker rarely falters. Negative feedback is motivational, and the Maker's journey often provides a larger framework, illuminating the arduous path ahead. Models: Richard Branson, Founder of Virgin Group. James Dyson, Inventor, Industrial Designer, Founder of Dyson Vacuum.

Perry Klebahn was one of the lucky ones, a young man who entered a university program designed to awaken budding product designers. Tall, lanky and athletic, with a direct demeanor, Perry had earned his bachelor's in physics at Wesleyan, and enrolled in the mechanical engineering master's program at Stanford. During the winter of his second year of graduate school Perry became intrigued by Design Garage, otherwise known as 116C. Less about theory and more about doing, the class was inspired by David Kelley, the charismatic founder of IDEO, the celebrated Palo Alto innovation and design firm with a golden touch – key to the success of dozens of hot tech products. Kelley was famous for his firm's early, pivotal work for premier Silicon Valley companies, not the least of them Apple.

Candidates for Design Garage would meet during the fall with one of Kelley's influential early IDEO staffers, Dennis Boyle, and explore potential ideas for new projects, only after this stage becoming eligible to apply. The students accepted into the course would spend the spring under the thrice weekly tutelage of Boyle, along with regular long weekly reviews with Kelley. The year was

1990, and it's hard to understate just how radical this approach was for those pre-Internet days. No one talked about innovation. Design thinking was not yet on the map. Stanford's celebrated and soon to be globally imitated d.school — integrating business, law, medicine, the social sciences and humanities into more traditional engineering and product design — would not be founded for more than 14 years.

That winter Perry drove up to Lake Tahoe, the Bay Area's winter playground. He was the odd man out. Pained by an old ankle injury, he couldn't join his buddies skiing or snowboarding. By chance, he found some snowshoes in the cabin, and decided on a lark to give it a try. Much to his surprise, he discovered that they were fashioned out of wood. Out on the snow he felt unsteady and kept slipping.

These pains sang to Perry like opportunities. As a mechanical engineer, he saw at a glance that snowshoes were still firmly stuck in the backwoods. The major improvements in light materials and flexible construction introduced in bicycles, cars, and airplanes during the latter part of the 20th century were strikingly absent from snowshoes. By now it was January. Perry had to come up with a project for Kelley's Design Garage, and he thought: snowshoes. He wasn't really sure how he'd redesign them, but he dove in. He knew how to make stuff: "It became these cycles of rapid-build on Monday, Tuesday and Wednesday," he said. Then he'd drive at the end of the week to the Sierras and test out his latest prototypes in the snow. "It was super fun," he said. "It evolved from making this thing quickly lighter and faster." Perry cobbled together aluminum tubing with a range of solid decking surfaces. Realizing that traction was essential to a superior on-snow experience, he began experimenting with bindings and a heel cleat.

Perry, as we'll soon see, was not a typical student. He had a knack for making stuff, a burning natural tenacity, and the advantage of the structured, design- and market-focused techniques he'd gleaned in Stanford's Design Garage. To his mind this wasn't just a class project. Perry was making snowshoes, and he thought that if he put his mind to it, he could make one heck of a snowshoe. "I approached it as a startup from day one. I wanted to have a company, and this was going to be it."

This enthusiasm was met with more than a little skepticism. Some fellow students criticized him for being too commercial, too focused on brand. But wasn't that the point? To make something people wanted to buy? Some faculty members wondered if he was moving too fast, ignoring fundamental design principles. "It doesn't look pretty. The design is not resolved," one professor told Perry during a review. "I want you to do the curriculum."

To which Perry had a ready retort: he had orders.

The Maker's Journey: Perry came of age in a simpler time, long before the Internet and smart phones. There was a purity in his Maker's compulsion to create, an authenticity in his engineer's training and stubborn need to launch a business out of something as tricky as designing and making a better snowshoe. Yet Perry's appeal is even broader. He will not be content to have one journey, one Awakening or one Shift. His world will radically change and he will have to adapt to stay relevant, to have the chance to one day found a remarkable Place that will be all about giving hundreds of others the chance to Launch, find the Money and Test.

The Leader
Allan Young
San Francisco, California

The Leader seeks meaning and a deeper human connection. Early on, the Leader may feel lost or search for a greater purpose. They share an eagerness to experiment in life and work on multiple planes that most would consider extreme. Naturally resistant to authority and formal structures, Leaders thrive when challenged, and exhibit a love of learning. Their mantra is: "create, build, move on to what's next."

Models: Oprah Winfrey, Media Mogul. Daniel Ek, Founder of Spotify.

Allan Young's parents were Chinese immigrants. His mother was a seamstress. His father juggled two jobs, stocking the shelves of a grocery, and working in a hardware store until late. Their work ethic didn't sink in. Allan was a screw-up. "I wanted to have fun instead of sit in class," he said. "I'd cut school. Go shoot hoops, or hang out at the Chinatown library." Yet his fondness for rebellion included a strong streak of intellectual curiosity. In the third grade, he learned to code in BASIC, and loved reading. But computers were for nerds. So he made "a conscious decision to play sports, to be a gangster." Allan learned the trick of swiftly pulling down the latch on the newspaper vending machines with a quick flip of the wrist. He saved a lot of quarters. Sure he read the sports, but he also pored over the business pages. Allan had a serious demeanor. He had a chiseled face, proud chin, intent eyes. His eyeglasses gave him a bookish bent, and he took advantage of the opportunity. He'd wander into a nearby Walden Books and stealthily wander back out with comic books and non-fiction books, business and tech magazines, from *Forbes* to *The Red Herring* and *The Industry Standard*. About the only thing Allan didn't steal was fiction. He wanted to read about real people. "I wanted to learn how to think, to learn about guys doing stuff out in the real world." He wasn't so keen on normal schoolwork. His high school GPA hovered at a dismal 1.8. Often, he'd just leave Chinatown, and wander the city streets.

One day, having ducked into a luxury San Francisco hotel to avail himself of the facilities, he noticed a conference going on and poked his head in. "This older gentleman was talking in front of a group of people," recounted Allan. "He was a speaker. People were crowding around him, asking about the boards he sat on, the stocks he invested in." Allan stood on the periphery and listened, patiently waiting his turn. He couldn't know this yet, but this was the moment the future leader would be brave, go deep in his search of knowledge, and his own destiny. When his time came he had a simple, extraordinary question: "How can I be like you?"

The man took the measure of this boy who'd clearly crashed his event, and then peppered him with queries. "Are you in school? Have you taken the SATs? What are your scores?"

The boy answered truthfully, and the man looked at him and said straight away: "You'll never be like me."

Allan was taken aback by his bluntness. "You don't come from the right background," the man continued. "You'll never make it. Your only shot is to learn a little bit about discipline. More importantly, leadership. You should join the military."

The words were tough but the man had a message, and Allan realized that he was being both direct and generous. Don't get caught up in all the "Rah, rah, and indoctrination of the military," the man said. "Spend time observing the leaders. Take in the different types. See what's effective. See how you feel toward them. Just watch it, watch it in slow motion."

Allan listened and thanked the man, and later, as he thought about the chance encounter, he reflected that the man never told him to acquire a skill, such as learning how to fix trucks or airplanes. He was just telling him to sign up, and study the leaders. "If you can learn from that, then find an opportunity to practice leadership," the man said. "Then you might have a shot at being successful."

The Leader's Journey: All too often we imagine we'll be transformed by a mythical light bulb aha moment that sends us hurtling forward. But Allan, like so many of us, first had to climb out of a dark hole. He came from a working class family with no history of higher education. He was on the verge of dropping out of high school. But this one chance encounter would spin him in a new direction, one that would require sacrifice, and the adoption of a rigorous philosophy focused on radical self-education and on taking on the mantle and responsibility of a Leader.

The Conductor
Carlos Muela
University of San Francisco

The Conductor designs novel experiences, quickly grasping the potential of creating a "network effect." They bring an innate tendency to think big, to explore how to build models that scale. Skilled at cross-pollinating with other experts to expand their reach, Conductors are constantly searching for more building blocks to add to their growing platforms, and aspire to share their passion. Models: Marc Benioff, Salesforce CEO, outspoken philanthropist and pioneer of Software as a Service (SaaS) cloud-based tech. Ben Silbermann, Pinterest Co-Founder.

Carlos Muela was expected to take over his father's business, and in another place and time, that most certainly would have been his fate. His father owned two restaurants, and there was every reason to think that he would follow in his footsteps. A native of Madrid, Muela senior had opened Picaro and Esperpento in San Francisco's Mission District decades ago, a classic tale of an immigrant making good through old-fashioned initiative and hard work.

By the age of eight Carlos was already a fixture in his father's two bustling tapas restaurants, cleaning up and making himself useful. By fourteen he was a waiter, and by seventeen, a manager. There was no reason to think he would choose another path. He'd grown up in the sleepy, working class town of Martinez, more than an hour away by car from San Francisco. But Carlos wanted more. He aspired to achieve something his father had never had the opportunity to do, to go to college, and something told him that the place he studied mattered more than the school. Carlos had the face of a Madrileño. He had dark, thick hair and as he became a man, favored a beard or goatee. Stocky, with warm, friendly eyes, his rugged and simple clothes expressed his earnest modesty.

Carlos enrolled at the University of San Francisco in large part because he was attracted by the energy he felt when he worked at the family's restaurants, the vibrant, international buzz of the city. At USF he majored in hospitality but also a brand-new discipline just catching on, called entrepreneurship. Carlos wasn't like other students. He logged 40+ hours a week managing the family's restaurants, doing bar inventory, buying supplies, coordinating "the staff and flow of the night – 200 people with reservations – planning out the entire evening," all while somehow finding the time to attend and pass his classes.

Carlos could handle pressure. He also had dreams. By the time he neared graduation, he knew that he "wasn't going to be doing" what his parents had done. "I had a million ideas, and my father had his crazy ones." Father and son didn't talk sports. They talked of the next big thing in food. Of creating a San Francisco-based twist on the Mercado de San Miguel, Madrid's famous prototypical food court. "One of our many ideas was that we should do a market hall," said Carlos, who after he graduated from USF considered leasing a huge 20,000-square-foot space and slicing it up into tiny units to be subleased to small vendors. But the risky, capital-intensive nature of the business scared them off.

What about a sangria bar in the Mission, featuring a wild assortment of wine cocktails and Latin American beers? Carlos hired an architect to create some renderings, but ultimately decided that concept too had its limitations. He began to shift toward a stronger model with far greater potential. Food trucks were just starting to take off, and by chance, a friend had an empty lot in San Francisco's Mission District, and offered him a bargain lease. Sensing opportunity, Carlos began frequenting Off the Grid events in Fort Mason and various Bay Area farmers' markets, the festival-styled gatherings for food trucks. He talked to food truck vendors, and learned something that surprised him: "There were all these food trucks with nowhere to go." Despite the supposed boom, San Francisco's few dozen food trucks were struggling. Contrary to popular belief they couldn't just drive around town and pull over on any street to serve customers. City regulations required them to operate on private property, and to keep the wheels turning they needed more days than the farmers' markets and Off the Grid events could provide.

Due to zoning issues, Carlos knew his friend's empty lot in the Mission wouldn't fly, but he found an abandoned lot at 11th and Harrison. The year was 2011, the space on the periphery of what would soon become the center of the tech explosion in San Francisco's SoMa district. On the surface it was a disaster, filled with decrepit old U-Haul trucks, "homeless people, huge rats, garbage, and strung-out drug addicts." Yet Carlos also noted that it was across from a cavernous parking lot for several big box stores, and near the hot tech firms Zynga, RDIO and Pinterest. Unlike the Mission district property, this lot was zoned for industrial use, a big advantage. Carlos had an idea for a novel open-air food concept. Not a restaurant. Not a sangria bar. Not the Mercado de San Miguel. Something no one had tried before in this city famous for foodies. A permanent park designed just for food trucks.

The Conductor's Journey: Carlos shows us clearly that we don't have to do what our parents did — whether they are doctors, lawyers, accountants, or in his case, restaurant owners. Nor do we have to rebel. Carlos will deftly parlay the advantage and momentum of being a subject matter expert. Steeped in the business of food, Carlos smartly studied not just hospitality but entrepreneurship in college. And not just anywhere. In San Francisco because he senses it's his Place. The Bay Area has thousands of independent restaurant owners. But Carlos will be the one to innovate, to break free of the traditional track to orchestrate a revolution in food.

The Outsider
Daniel Lewis
Palo Alto, California

A "beginner's mind" offers the advantage of curiosity, ignorance, even the armor of arrogance. Outsiders have nothing invested in the standard practice, current product, or status quo. They boldly assume that they can do better, even if there's no reason to think they're anything but amateurs. They simply don't know any other way. Sometimes the best opportunity is staring you right in the face, within your chosen industry or field, or just when you're getting started. The Outsider absorbs everything they can in a product or service with an inherently objective eye, and a forward lean, as if it's inevitable that they'll be the one to hit it out of the park. Models: Brian Chesky, Founder of Airbnb. Tony Hsieh, CEO of Zappos.

Daniel Lewis's parents were lawyers and the odds were high that he too would one day practice law. He'd worked one summer at his father's boutique law firm before heading off to earn a degree in international studies at Johns Hopkins, and then quickly landed a plum job at a think tank in the nation's capital. Daniel wanted to make a difference in energy and climate policy, and felt he was in the right place, working with the right people. But after a couple of years he began to question the reach of his individual impact. "It's a very big ecosystem, there's a lot of ways that policy gets made and shaped," he recounted. "So it was becoming hard to figure out how I was putting points on the board."

Daniel was competitive, a college baseball player, a pitcher no less, a young man who thought in terms of tangible accomplishments, measuring success in a pitch, strikeout, or win. Tall, with tousled hair, a square jaw and a dimpled chin, Daniel had classic athletic good looks. He applied to Stanford Law School, was accepted, and began class in the fall of 2009. He figured he'd end up a litigator like his father, or maybe since Stanford was smack in the middle of Silicon Valley, work in the emerging field of clean tech. But he also had a playful, creative streak. Within his first few weeks on the campus he toyed with creating a consumer product to help people select wines, even making some calls and talking to experts in the wine business.

The momentum stuck. During his second year he found a serious problem to tackle. It struck Daniel that the Stanford Law library's digital tools seemed nearly identical to what he'd seen at his dad's firm ten years before. Here in Silicon Valley, why were they stuck in this time warp, he wondered? All this great technology on the Internet, but why not in legal research? It was a problem he knew firsthand from researching case law for class. "The pain of it was that you could spend hours, and have very little confidence that you got the right answer, that you'd looked at everything that needed to be looked at." Out in the real world, he knew, this could mean the difference between winning and losing a case. Daniel had a vision for something radically different, a "new kind of research that would be more visual, more data-driven."

This had nothing, and perhaps everything, to do with attending law school. He saw his idea as a hobby, like the wine app that never went anywhere, or even the softball team he'd started at the think tank. Daniel liked to be busy, exploring new ideas, and he figured that at Stanford University, of all places, he might be able to get some answers.

He scoured Stanford's computer science course listings, picked out some professors, and began randomly showing up at office hours. The professors were surprised. Daniel wasn't enrolled in their classes. He was truly an outsider. He knew nothing about computer science. But still, after a little initial confusion about what he was doing there, the professors offered help. "I would show up, talk with them, and they would send me a couple of research papers related to searching legal cases or doing natural language processing." Soon, Daniel was emailing post docs and IBM researchers all over the world, setting up phone calls "to learn what they were doing, and whether they'd carried their work forward at all." All while studying law.

Next, he explored what was happening on the customer end. "I'd call the main line of a law firm, and ask to talk to the librarian," he said. He'd probe how they felt about the tools they used. Did they hate them or love them? Wish there was a better technology? He told his subjects that he was a Stanford Law student doing research (which, strangely enough, was true). "I was getting a sense for whether there was any interest. Was I the only one feeling this pain?" The beginner was quickly zeroing in on the opportunity, and uncovering the obstacles to innovation. There was a reason there had been a lack of technological advances in legal research. LexisNexis and Westlaw had successfully carved out an effective duopoly, a reality that Daniel saw in how the law firms he was interviewing felt about the company's products, and their high pricing for the over one million lawyers in the US. "So that was new to me, I was learning the context of why these tools hadn't changed much, and what the businesses that ran them looked like."

The summer before his final year of law school, Daniel teamed up with a friend studying at Berkeley's Haas School of Business. "We started thinking about putting this down on paper. Okay, there's some interesting technology out there, there's a customer pain. But is there actually a valid product that you could build? What does the revenue model look like?" Daniel had no business asking such big, fundamental questions, but the beautiful thing was that he simply didn't know any better. And he was starting to sense that this was becoming more than a hobby.

The Outsider's Journey: Far too often we are blind to an opportunity staring us in the face. Our world. Daniel demonstrates the value of adopting the beginner's mindset. He doesn't know what he doesn't know. He doesn't care if most people would think that it's crazy for someone who never practiced law or wrote a line of code to imagine re-inventing the technology a million lawyers use to research cases. He shows us the edge in taking an Outsider's view, even if you don't happen to be an Outsider. Strangely, more is often possible when you are on the outside, looking in, and Daniel's curiosity and naivety will help him in ways he can't envision.

The Accidental
Mait Müntel
Tallinn, Estonia

One small step followed by another can take you a long way. Accidentals are distinguished initially by their lack of formal intent. They may appear to be hobbyists, but they take it up a notch, obsessively tinkering or compiling knowledge about a subject until they've unwittingly built something with a life of its own. They rarely plan to launch a company. Indeed, the Accidental is quite often content in their chosen work. Until the accident — when they discover they're onto something pretty darn interesting. Some new idea they just keep coming back to, and then it snowballs and they realize, they just have to start a company. Models: Craig Newmark, Craigslist Founder. Stewart Butterfield, Founder of Flickr and Slack.

Mait Müntel's first focus was on the stars. The Tartu Observatory was founded in his native Estonia in 1824, equipped with a nine-inch Fraunhofer refractor, at the time the largest achromatic telescope in the world. Several legendary Estonian and European astronomers would take up residence at the famed Tartu Observatory, men who mapped Mars and played a critical role in unlocking the large-scale structure of the universe, and Mait hoped to follow in their celestial steps. He had a gift for math, and began studying astronomy and physics at the University of Tartu. During his second year, one of his toughest professors challenged him after he'd excelled in a difficult exam: "I want to see you as a physicist."

Mait was touched by that early vote of confidence and fully embraced his future as a scientist. While working on his doctorate, he heard about the legendary CERN laboratory, soon to house the world's largest particle accelerator, and arrived in Switzerland in the summer of 2004, making the switch from nuclear to particle physics, "from studying the biggest things to the smallest things." Mait was part of the core CERN team of physicists who began writing programs to simulate particle collisions even before the Hadron accelerator was built. It was the first real programming Mait had ever done. These were programs to simulate what happens during millions of particle collisions – 600 million times a second, "and millions and billions of tracks" – programs to prove the fundamental structure of the universe, one particle at a time.

Mait spent his summers at CERN, gradually staying for longer and longer periods until eventually he was living at the lab near Geneva, Switzerland – in French-speaking territory. Sturdy with a wavy mop of light brown hair and thick glasses, Mait was enthusiastic and good natured. He was at heart a considerate guy, and was acutely embarrassed that he did not speak the local language. It was, as he recalls, "A very personal feeling." He had grown up during the Soviet occupation of Estonia and it had bothered him that the nonnative Russian population had never learned the local language. "It was kind of an attitude," he said, and not a welcome one. And now here he was living and working in Switzerland. "And I'm not learning French. I'm being as impolite as the Russians. It kind of tortured me."

Mait's need was elemental. Develop some ingenious method to learn French quickly. But for all of Mait's gifts in math and physics, he had never shown promise in languages. After ten years of Russian in school, he'd learned almost nothing. His English had improved – it was the language spoken at CERN – but still he struggled. One day he thought to himself, *If computing processing power can be used to find unknown particles, maybe it could be harnessed to teach a language.* To nearly everyone else on the planet this might have been an idle thought, quickly forgotten. But Mait was a remarkable scientist who had no compunction about exploring an unproven and extraordinary concept. The celebrated Higgs boson project had ended, and he had a little extra time on his hands, and the tremendous computational power of CERN's supercomputers at his fingertips. He wondered:

What, theoretically, would be the shortest possible time needed to learn a language, if we could optimize everything? He ran some hypothetical estimates, and came up with a radically low figure, under 200 hours. It seemed too good to be true.

The Accidental's Journey: So many things in our lives are unplanned. Yet there is latent potential and promise in the unexpected. One could never have predicted that Mait would toy with creating an amazing new AI, machine learning language program. Fate plays such a large part in our lives — chance encounters, upbringing, culture, city and circumstance. Mait will show us that someone with no business jumping into a startup, has more potential than we might ever imagine.

The Athlete
Joel Heath
Vail, Colorado

People grow in different ways. Athletes learn from movement and the unpredictability of the wild. The Athlete loves a contest and a challenge: they climb rock faces, venture into fearsome surf, slalom down perilous slopes. They relish preparing for the... unexpected. Adapt, recover, pivot is their mantra. Athletic entrepreneurs intuit the connections between seemingly diverse activities, building new opportunities around what they love: motion. Models: Yvon Chouinard, Founder of Patagonia. Nick Woodman, Founder of GoPro.

Joel Heath was an athlete who exuded cool, a competitive swimmer and outdoor enthusiast who grew up in beautiful Boulder, Colorado, with a deep love of the outdoors. Upon earning his business degree he had a simple goal: to get into traditional ski mountain management by taking a job at Vail's ski school. But then, a chance internship at the local tourism bureau gave him a taste of a new, fast developing trend. Adventure sports were quickly rising in popularity, and Joel spied an opportunity to entirely reimagine the mountain experience, launching his first company, Untraditional Marketing, Inc.

No one had done an event quite like the one Joel dreamed up for Vail. He took niche sports and activities such as rock climbing, kayaking, adventure racing, mountain biking, and trail running – 27 different events – and threw them all together into a wild mix called the Mountain Games. "It was cool to see," said Joel. "We just kind of jammed a lot of different but similar people into the same town."

The Mountain Games was all about cross-pollination. For the first time, outdoor enthusiasts could witness a myriad of sports and radical athletes in one iconic, sprawling mountain setting. He was tapping a pain with a novel product. Mainstream companies finally had a viable means to sponsor adventure-related sports, and Joel was neatly positioned to capitalize on that demand. His brand and promotional agency attracted major clients – just as the Mountain Games quickly rose to become the world's largest outdoor adventure event, broadcast on NBC and CBS. Joel, meanwhile, was carving out a natural philosophy around work and engagement, starting with the concept that work and play don't have to be separate. He began to hold staff "chair" meetings for Untraditional on the brief chairlift rides up the mountain. "We shortened conversations," he said. "It was a healthy way to dialog." They worked hard, while also maintaining a "six-inch powder rule", where there was an understanding about their shared passion. The workday could be truncated when the snow was great.

Surrounded by Vail's spectacular mountains Joel felt the conflict between traditional business culture and nature. "Business seemed to want to make the world flat," he remembered thinking. Everything was about safety. Chaining people down. Locking their feet to the floor. Not moving for hours. This traditional approach to work struck Joel as outdated, especially given Untraditional's success. Instability was where he saw dynamic growth.

"You know, true flatness makes you sedentary, and a sedentary life is a dangerous one. It's like a river that doesn't flow, like the person who says, 'I think I'm gonna stay home.' And the same things held true in my mind for how we work, so I just set out on a journey with a purpose to help set the world in motion."

Joel couldn't know it at the time, but his years in the wild, inventing and launching the Mountain Games, were preparing him for an entirely different sort of entrepreneurial challenge. One that would soon lead him to probe a simple, yet fundamental way people might shake free of the drudgery of office routine. And stand up for themselves.

The Athlete's Journey: In life and work, we sometimes forget that we're physical, spiritual beings, influenced as much by passion as logic, plan-

ning and money. Joel's path will remind us that we don't need to be an Athlete to understand how intangibles can inspire us to get moving. To listen to what our bodies and gut are telling us. Joel's first big wins in marketing the Mountain Games put him in the eye of a storm that had been brewing for years. Smart phones, the Internet and wireless technology ushered in a new era for the mobile worker. But Joel was just the man to see that, technology aside, our bodies are often pretty much still stuck. And he had an idea to set us free.

The Visionary
Risto Lähdesmäki
Helsinki, Finland

Visionaries see far ahead. Their passion drives them to explore emerging fields. They may initially lack the words to fully describe what they're doing, but that doesn't stop them. They're radically creative experimenters, painfully honest, and frequently mistake-prone. Which makes perfect sense because they've got a hard shell. They're masters at learning from failure. Visionaries are charismatic, bursting with conviction, natural salespeople with a gift for attracting followers. Models: Steve Jobs, Apple Computer Founder. Seth Godin, Author.

Risto Lähdesmäki's childhood hobby was playing with his Atari. He was born into a generation of young Finnish boys during the heyday of mobile phone giant Nokia, a coding-crazy culture that helped lay the foundation for top mobile and gaming firms, giving rise to a wealth of techies, graphic artists, and gamers. "When I was in seventh grade, for some reason I really had to have a computer. I learned coding," recalled the Helsinki native. "It seemed as if I was literally 24/7, for two years, in front of my Atari 26-inch black-and-white screen coding in BASIC."

Coding as a boy connected Risto with his talent for drawing and art. Born in 1972, Risto was coming of age at that seminal moment when PCs and Macs caught fire. At thirteen, he wrote and published a small computer drawing program. Music came naturally. He started playing in a band but lacked the right instrument. Girls seemed to favor guys who played keyboard, so Risto worked to earn enough money to buy one. He took on jobs as a freelance art director, creating logos and corporate graphics. He bought his first keyboard. Music was about taking chances, improvising. He learned to read music and play popular songs, but never "got much enjoyment out of playing someone else's notes. Rather taking forks and improvising and playing."

Inspiration came from a college professor who opened his eyes to the power of "expressing himself through art." Risto was studying to be a teacher, and thought it a noble profession, but it wasn't his path. He dropped out and plugged into the Mac and Internet revolution. By the mid 90s he was creating web sites for clients, loving how his interests dovetailed through art, web design and coding. Art and the computer interface were intertwined from the start, and it was natural for him "to get a first touch of human-centric design between the human being and computer through web pages."

In the late 90s, Risto worked with an ad agency in Helsinki, and around the millennium it dawned on him that he wanted to be an entrepreneur. He didn't like the term. He hadn't set out to be one. He didn't really have the background. No one in his family had forged their own path. He wasn't even sure what it meant to be an entrepreneur. What he did know was that he "didn't want to have to go and ask permission."

Risto was one of those young men who grew into his good looks. Broad shouldered, with thick brows and a solid nose, he had the kind of face you didn't forget. Risto had a knowing, puckish smile that exuded charisma, and a solid, novel idea. Art, design, and the computer came naturally to him. Risto wanted to connect that with deep research. A fresh understanding of users' wants and needs. The term user interface was new to Finland, but it spoke to him: "I want to be on the screen, I want to be creating something beautiful, easy to use, useful on digital."

Risto was intrigued by something sorely missing. The profession of user interface design did not yet exist, and he felt there was a larger opportunity to create a new kind of company. Not just randomly building web pages, but digging deeper into the fundamental opportunity of what was an inherently interactive and data rich new medium. And so, Risto began studying and observing computer users around the world, focusing on that one simple but critical element missing all too often between man and machine – empathy.

The Visionary's Journey: Our search for purpose and meaning propel us through life. Aiming high, perhaps even for an ideal, can help illuminate and fortify your path. Risto might have been a schoolteacher or a talented, traditional designer. His isolation in Finland should have narrowed his options. But Risto was a Visionary and as we'll soon see, he will courageously imagine and realize an extraordinary future. He will show us the value of setting outrageous personal goals, of pushing beyond what seems possible, proving that only the timid are constrained by fate or geography.

The Guardian
Karoli Hindriks
Pärnu, Estonia

Guardians protect and liberate people by taking down barriers or confronting inequities. Products and services are causes and movements to Guardians. They seek out an underlying authentic purpose that inspires a passionate search for success, and the deepest possible level of commitment. Models: Malala Yousafzai, education activist and founder of the Malala Fund. Patrick O. Brown, molecular biologist and founder of Impossible Foods.

Karoli Hindriks didn't have the luxury of growing up in the red hot entrepreneurial centers of San Francisco, New York, or London. She lacked the advantage of Place. This was Pärnu, Estonia, in the 1980s, at the time under the heavy shadow of the Soviet Union. "I call it the dark side of the world," she said. "Private enterprises were forbidden. You can't travel, there was barely food. It was an exercise in innovation for each family just to have dinner on the table because if you went to the grocery store it was all empty." But then, when she was just eight years old, tiny Estonia, with a population of just 1.5 million, declared independence from the Soviet Union.

Karoli had grown up in a locked-down world without possibility, and now suddenly she "had the privilege to actually experience the open and free world, yet still remembering and appreciating the dark side." By chance her high school had a Junior Achievement Program. One of the exercises was to create a student company, and to her surprise, she was elected president of the new venture. Inspired to be put in such a position of trust, she immediately began brainstorming. It was October, the brutal Estonian winter beginning its long and dark six-month reign. "People are not visible. There are a lot of bike accidents on the roads, and the reflectors are ugly and plastic and don't really look cool." That pain led to a Guardian-inspired epiphany with a marketing twist: "I thought what if we make reflectors that are fashionable that teenagers like me would actually want to wear?"

She excitedly told her father. Another man might have told her that it was silly, or impossible. Teenagers did not start companies in Estonia during the 1990s. Instead, he was supportive. "What a great idea. Why don't you go to the patent office?" Karoli had no concept of a patent office, but soon found out. "You have this 16-year-old girl coming in," she recalled. "For them it was also a big surprise. They did all the research on whether it was a unique idea, for free – because they were excited for young people, excited about us doing something."

Karoli Hindriks became the youngest inventor in Estonia's history, and wasted no time in getting down to business. The flaxen-haired pixie pounded the pavement to meet with sales leads. As she dove into her student company, her dreams soared higher. Growing up, she had been captivated by the American sitcom *Saved by the Bell*, a series that followed a group of high school students. Karoli wanted to "see how America works," wanted to study in America. She was offered three scholarships, but the price was still too high for her parents. She went to Pärnu's mayor seeking a scholarship. The town couldn't sponsor her either, but the mayor happened to be part of the local Rotary Club, and it just so happened that he was preparing to visit their sister-city. In America, he made a public plea for the girl from Pärnu with a dream. Karoli soon found her way to a high school in New Hampshire, sponsored by the family of a refugee from Estonia, who had escaped during World War II and always wanted to do something for the tiny country.

It was one of those pivotal experiences that change a life. In New England, Karoli was frequently invited to speak before large groups about her student company. Her confidence blossomed. "That was kind of an exciting start. I loved the energy from the 'Yes, you can!' American attitude," she said. She came back to Estonia, and decided she wanted to build a real business out of it – for profit. For real. She was 17, about to enter university. Karoli Hindriks was just getting started.

The Guardian's Journey: Sometimes one woman's actions can encapsulate the heart of a nation. Karoli's story parallels that of Estonia itself, which came into its own following the Soviet-era occupation, when government leaders made a decision to start fresh as a digital nation, shedding the antiquated legacy systems of their oppressors. Karoli learned determination and resourcefulness from her own parents' grit. Her protective instincts were baked in early, and will guide her career decisions throughout many upcoming transitions. Success has a way of generating more success, and Karoli will show us the importance of honing our self-reliance no matter the obstacles.

The Evangelist
Uwe Diegel
Bophuthatswana, South Africa

The Evangelist has an uncanny ability to fan interest in his passions. He's a natural at spinning the story behind the product before it's even created. He knows how to strike just the right points to touch hearts and move minds. Models: Vint Cerf, DARPA manager, ICANN founder, American Internet pioneer, recognized as one of "the fathers of the Internet." Esther Dyson, Author, Speaker, Investor.

Uwe Diegel was born in Dunedin, New Zealand, hardly a city or nation celebrated for entrepreneurs. His father was a mathematician, a profession that would take them on an academic tour of duty to Germany, Alabama, Quebec, and then Durban, South Africa. His mother exhibited an intense European love of language, culture and music. She was a linguist, a translator who spoke nearly a dozen languages, descended from the family of Audemars Piguet, the legendary Swiss watchmakers.

Uwe's childhood was dominated by his mother's clockwork demand that he and his siblings train daily in music and language. "There were five of us. We were the Von Trapp family. Everybody had to play a musical instrument," recalled Uwe, the fourth child. "Every morning between 6:00 and 7:00 we all had to practice with music for one hour before going to school." After school, his mother would have the children read literature and recite poetry. "My mother would come home and say, 'All right, kids. This year we're doing 17th century French literature!'" And then there was dance. "She had this obsession with our having a European culture. So we all had to be in ballet."

Uwe studied ballet for 17 years. The music stuck. Uwe began playing piano at five and was good at it. His career took off when he was 14, shortly after the family's arrival in South Africa. Uwe studied music more intently, and became a concert pianist, eventually receiving a degree in music from the University of Cape Town. Uwe had the hair of an 80s-era rockstar, and the proud posture of a man who owned the stage. He performed throughout Africa and then later in Europe and Canada, often doing five concerts a week. By the age of 25, he'd spent nearly half his life as a professional musician. Then one day while roughhousing with his brother something happened he hadn't planned. He broke his arm. He had it fixed, and played for a while as an accompanist, but then came the pain. His ulnar nerve was rubbing against the bone, and eventually the nerve snapped and his career as a musician was finished.

Teaching music at the University of Cape Town Uwe met Lily Lin, a woman who had immigrated from Taiwan. They began dating, and every summer they'd go to Lily's parents' place in Bophuthatswana. The family had a small dairy factory, and Uwe began helping out. Finally, one summer, Lily's father said: "Well, why don't you come and work at the factory?" Uwe resigned from the university, came to Bophuthatswana, and soon took over the factory. While doing research he discovered that black Africans don't drink milk but instead a thick soured dairy concoction called Amasi because it's easier for them to digest.

He was staring right at a classic pain point, a product gap for an entire culture. While on his honeymoon in Taiwan, Uwe happened to learn about BongBong Ice – ice cream machines "which make low-lactose milk in plastic tubes." He imported the machines to Africa and reinvented the process to fill the tubes with low-lactose ice cream. By then, Uwe was in his late 20s. Uwe no longer missed his past life as a musician. He'd discovered that he had a gift for marketing, for selling concepts to people, an ability to tap the well of knowledge gifted to him in his homespun renaissance education, and perhaps most of all, a hunger to explore a completely different kind of creativity.

The Evangelist's Journey: One of the core tenets of growth and leadership is the importance of studying famous success stories. People who've knocked it out of the park — not once, but again and again. Uwe is just starting out, but he will grow into that classic model seen in so many great entrepreneurs, the Evangelist. And his story will carry more weight because he set out on this course after the tragedy of suddenly having his music career ripped away. Fortunately for us, Uwe is about to apply his performer's bravado to prototyping and marketing products, demonstrating how fluidity, experience, and the zeal of an Evangelist can heighten your odds of success.

The Collaborator
Joe Boggio
Three Rivers, Michigan

Sometimes the quiet ones make the most impact. They may be in the back of the room, but they're listening, puzzling out how everything fits together. The cards may seem stacked against them. They may grow up in the worst place. Lack all the usual advantages. Their psychology and temperament seem wrong for the challenge. But from their angle on the sidelines, they take in the key players, big picture, and quietly get stuff done. Eschewing the spotlight, the Collaborator chooses instead to grow into a masterful connector who leads by maximizing talents. Models: Bill Hewlett and David Packard, Founders of HP. Ray Dalio, Founder of Bridgewater Associates, "Principles" Author.

Joe Boggio grew up in Three Rivers, a small town in southwestern Michigan, with brothers and sisters nearly a generation older, "so when I came along it was almost as if I was an only child." Joe's grandfather traced his roots to Piedmont, Italy, and his father grew up on a street in town nicknamed Spaghetti Avenue. When Joe was 13, his father retired from the Navy and moved the family to Jones, Michigan. There was a gas station and a flashing light, and that was it for miles in any direction. That isolation helped make Joe "a really, really shy kid who didn't like being a shy kid." He saw trade school as a solution to his social fears, a way out. His junior year, Joe would endure the first three hours of his morning at the local high school, and then take an hour bus ride to spend the afternoon in a simple lab, learning the electrician's trade. "I thought, OK, sweet, I'm going to be able to hide, you know, ride out my last two years of high school."

Then he met John Capella, his trade school teacher. A Marine helicopter gunner in Vietnam, "Mr. C" demanded discipline with a direct method of enforcement. A stack of toilet paper rolls on his desk – just in case you weren't paying attention. "He would whip one of these rolls of toilet paper at you," said Joe. "You were not going to get hurt, but he came in hot."

Along with firing rolls of toilet paper, Mr. C cared deeply about his charges. He quickly saw through Joe's shyness and told him how it was going to be. "I'm not going to let you get away with this," he told the boy. "You've got more in you, and I'm going to pull it out of you."

No one had ever talked to Joe this way. Not his parents. Not his friends. Definitely not his other teachers. "You've got to make a life choice. You can either be afraid, and at the back of the pack, or you can decide to be at the cutting edge." The discipline wrapped in compassion spoke to Joe. This teacher who cared and saw something more than his tremendous shyness and fear. "He changed me, and challenged me, in so many ways," said Joe. "I started to want to make him proud of me."

It was like flipping a switch. Joe's wiring changed, in part because his mentor brought more than just talk. Mr. C made Joe class president and pressed him into a prominent role, appointing him to lead class each morning. It was an early glimpse into his potential as a team player, a Collaborator. No longer content with being in the back, Joe moved up front, confronting his shyness, finally exploring what he really wanted to do with his life. The chance to lead. That was inspiring. Joe had grown up hearing stories of courage and honor from his Navy father. Now he had a new role model who was also a veteran. Mr. C was a die-hard Marine, and Joe wanted more. He stopped in at a recruitment office. He was 17. Scared but 100% in. "I had an agreement with the recruiter that the very next day, Saturday morning, I would come back and sign up."

But first he had to tell his dad.

The Collaborator's Journey: Our futures are not solely determined by early advantages, the luck of being born into a prosperous family, the privilege of a top education. Such fortune wasn't in Joe's favor, or maybe it was. His ex-Navy father was retired by the time he was a teen. The isolation of growing up in rural America fed Joe's natural introvert tendencies. But a mentor intervened before that pattern stuck. And Joe would develop a Marine-like discipline toward reaching out, toward seeking and honing the essential tools of collaboration, both with individuals and corporations, reminding us that we cannot do this alone, and that our Awakening is very much a team sport.

Takeaways:
Finding Your Awakening

There is no one way to Awaken. The Faces provide multiple paths for your crucial beginning. Who helps you discover your initial burst of inspiration?

Makers start with a prototype.
Leaders begin by studying leaders.
Outsiders trust in their "beginner's mind."
Accidentals embrace their obsessions.
Conductors vary the model — big, small or in between.
Athletes see motion as driving performance.
Guardians think of others first.
Evangelists begin with the story.
Collaborators start by connecting.
Visionaries lean around the bend.

The Shift

Some people scribble down business concepts in a notebook. Others on Post-its or a whiteboard. Joel penned his list on his bathroom mirror. He called it his shark tank. Five ideas staring back at him when he shaved in the morning, five ideas that every day he moved a little further along.

The Shift is a fundamental move from thinking to doing. Simply awakening is not enough. You can awaken and fall back to sleep. You can awaken but stay on the fence. You Shift when you move beyond talking about change, to a new phase where you take action.

Action brings confidence. The confidence to stand up to peers, friends and families who may try to thwart your quest. The Shift is marked by boldness, initiative, and curiosity. You start congregating with people who get it. Leaders and entrepreneurs in your chosen field who can teach and guide you. People who are also awake, proactive, and supportive.

The Shift is also where we begin to consider how to change lives, and the possibilities of scale, which at heart is why many people start a business or launch a startup, or for that matter, decide they need a better job, one with more challenges or greater rewards. There are a hundred easier, more predictable ways to make a good living, with far less risk. Things nearly always take longer than we think, hurdles often rise up that we haven't foreseen. For nine out of ten people, it's tough to Shift. You've never done this before. The time doesn't seem right, or your partner is wavering. For many of us those are reasons enough to hesitate. Or to buckle in and firmly grab the wheel.

Opportunities don't just fall off trees like ripe apples. You've got to sign up. Apply to a stimulating program or college. Hop on a plane. Budding entrepreneurs refuse to let their nationality or geography narrow their dreams. That boldness requires a radical shift in mindset.

At heart, you've got to make your own luck. The Shift comes in the audaciousness of changing your mindset. Following your inner compass to an unexpected break, a chance to bust out of a predictable, linear, and perhaps limited path. To choose risk and its thrilling possibilities.

The Maker

Perry Hits the Open Road

Design Garage had been more than a class to Perry Klebahn. The experience introduced him to a method, a new way of identifying market needs and prototyping products. And while many of his classmates were enthralled by the chance to study under David Kelley and Dennis Boyle of IDEO, in the main they took the safe, expected path. They did the work, earned good grades, and continued on with their exceptional lives as Stanford students, joining established, premier companies upon graduation. This was 1990, after all. Nobody was talking about entrepreneurs or innovation, on campus or anywhere else. Google, Facebook, and countless other hot tech companies were far off in the future, waiting for the web to be born.

Perry didn't know any better. He incorporated Atlas Snowshoes with Jim Klingbeil, an old high school buddy, setting up shop in his garage. His parents thought he was throwing away his life. They saw a bright son who had earned a physics degree from a prestigious college about to receive his master's in mechanical engineering at Stanford. Why in the world would he want to take on the tremendous financial and emotional risk of starting his own company? How could he possibly fashion a credible business out of a product as outdated and marginal as snowshoes?

But all that push-back merely rolled off Perry's back. He was blissfully free of any nagging self-doubt. The entrepreneur pokes his head into a new world and thinks *This is it! I've got the answer!* and Perry had the confidence to know he was onto something and charge boldly ahead. He wasn't seeking external validation, and certainly not from his parents or his peers. If anything, he yearned to prove them all wrong.

Perry was naïve and stubborn enough to think *why not go for it*, without setting his sights too far ahead. His initial, clunky snowshoe experience led him to believe that he could leap ahead of competitors by designing a far superior product. He was a born Maker. He put his head down and made stuff. By the end of Design Garage, Perry had created a good working prototype. He'd reached the precipice at which a lot of aspiring entrepreneurs back away, realizing there are easier paths, easier careers, easier ways to make a buck. Perry didn't blink. He plunked down $15,000 of his savings, and logged hours during the day as a part-time design consultant. At night, he and Klingbeil cobbled together snowshoes at an old wooden desk. The book *The Lean Startup* had yet to be written, its fast-prototyping and validated learning principles 21 years down the road. Perry had no mentors in this emerging world of founders and startups, no map for his entrepreneurial mindset. They made a bunch of snowshoes. They found an outfit that would paint Perry's old Chevy K5 Blazer with the Atlas name and logo for a bargain $100 – as long as it was yellow – and hit the open road. "We drove all over the West," said Perry. "We were driving fools. We drove to Aspen, Vail and Tahoe." They'd proven they had the imagination, energy, and skill to ideate, prototype and to make.

Now they just had to sell the darned things.

The Outsider
Daniel Switches Tracks

Entering his last year of law school, there was little expectation that Daniel would do anything more than the planned. Graduate, pass the bar, and step into a lucrative profession in the law. His parents were lawyers and he would be one too. But Daniel was at Stanford Law School. One of the magical things about Stanford wasn't just how easily you could catch the entrepreneurship bug. The university itself, as a living, breathing institution, was full of inspiring professors, classes, programs, and a collective can-do vibe that naturally sparked The Shift.

Daniel Lewis took a venture capital course during the fall of his final year at Stanford Law School that required him to write and pitch a business plan. He knew he couldn't do it alone. His friend at Berkeley couldn't participate. So he joined forces with Nik Reed, a fellow Stanford law student and business school grad with prior experience as a management consultant. The VC class was an ideal, early forum to shape their nascent idea. The professor had considerable experience with startups, VCs and the law, and that encouraging attitude so essential to a would-be entrepreneur during the fragile, early ideation stage. After they pitched to the class, the professor took them aside and told them: "You might be onto something."

Keeping going was the natural course at Stanford for the motivated. Daniel and Nik listened to their professor and entered a major campus-wide business plan competition. They were just one of 150 teams, but that winter and spring of 2012, they somehow found a way to carve out time from their intense law school studies to compete in a series of judging rounds to business school professors and venture capitalists.

They doubled down. One afternoon they arrived at Stanford's

famed d.school for the pre-class office hours for Launchpad, a collaborative, product design class. Launchpad was the place to go if you were itching to build your startup. The professors – themselves top graduates from Stanford and Harvard with experience in startups and venture capital – ran the course like an action-focused accelerator. To pass Launchpad, students had to come up with a promising product or service, formally incorporate, and then turn it into a thriving business. Which meant it was anything but the typical, academic entrepreneurship class. Though just in its third year, Launchpad already had an impressive track record of birthing successful companies. Just to be admitted into the class was considered an achievement.

Office hours formally began the second week of January, and ran right up until the first day of class, April 1, a test to see which teams had the Right Stuff. The crowd huddled around the professors on that first January afternoon was enough to intimidate Daniel and Nik: Stanford computer geeks, PhDs in the hard sciences, pre-meds, and grad students in business and design, each confidently pitching a product or service idea. Many were finishing up a masters or doctorate at Stanford and the professors made clear that Launchpad was only for those who were committed to launching their startups immediately after graduation in June.

"Think about Launchpad as an accelerator," the professors said to the assembled students. "It's not an academic effort. It's around launching to learn." Then, without further ado, they jumped in. A couple of students stepped up. The professors peppered them with three questions, illustrated on the whiteboard:

Who's your target customer?
What's your targeted pain point?
What's your key feature?

The first attempts were invariably too broad or fuzzy. They pressed the student to focus on a very specific target customer and need. Excuses were common: *We haven't built the website yet.... We haven't gotten the buttons to work yet.* That was the wrong approach. "Don't build the website," the professors would say, pointing out that the first task was to present a quick, primitive version of their offering to a potential customer. The rapid-fire, iterative process could be jarring. The professors' interactions abrupt. Most students brought a "write a business plan, build the website, study the market" academic style that had served them so well at Stanford, but at Launchpad was considered an anchor.

We only want to hear what you've done.
We don't care about the idea.
We care about the work you've done.
Do it, and sell it.

At times, staring down a reluctant Stanford student, who just a moment before had been supremely confident in their perfectly ascending academic career, the interchange resembled Yoda mentoring Luke Skywalker.

Don't try, there is only doing.
Find what you need to be doing, by doing.

The professors pushed the students to view these quick messy experiments as integral. To see prototyping as a fast track to create data. "You need to get your target users and deliver the service," they'd say. "See if you are solving a pain that matters. See if you can charge something for it."

Every once in a while, a team excelled. "We love the specificity!" the professors would exult when a student came back with a distinct "target feature" or "target need." Then they'd push to the next, key step: "Are you talking to potential users?" The answer might be promising – a team had talked to 25 people. But the "users" were fellow students, not potential customers. The professors wanted them to sell. "Where this class is unique is we do not espouse any more talking to the user without making the offer."

The rare teams with game got on it. They tracked down real customers, sold a primitive offering, and were rewarded with an even tougher assignment to complete in a few days. These were tests, and many teams struggled to shift from talking, planning, and cosmetic work, to selling.

Daniel and Nik were fish out of water, genuine Outsiders. Neither knew the first thing about the d.school, design thinking, entrepreneurship, or what it took to build sophisticated software. On the surface, all they had was a business plan: two law students trying to get into a class for which they appeared wholly unprepared. But taken from another vantage that might have been one reason to believe in them. Daniel and Nik had no business showing up to Launchpad office hours, and yet here they were, making an identity shift, taking on the mindset and actions of entrepreneurs.

The initial response was chilly. "Hey, we've never had law students before, we're a little skeptical," the professors told them bluntly. "It's not a course about creating a business plan. It's about actually prototyping and launching." Most students would have lost their nerve. Daniel and Nik were not easily dissuaded. Week after week, they kept coming to office hours, waiting their turn to spend a few minutes describing their idea. The professors wanted more: "Why don't you go out and create some paper prototypes and actually talk with some people?"

The Collaborator
Joe Starts a Club

Few of us start along the journey of entrepreneurship with the advantage of an Ivy League or Stanford education. Many first have to shift their outlook on a more fundamental level, resetting who they are and who they might be. Joe Boggio's hurdle was personal, that challenge Mr. C had thrown his way: *You've gotta make a life choice. You can either be afraid and at the back of the pack or you can decide to be on the cutting edge.* Joe embraced his teacher's tough love. He shifted. He put his back into it. And he found so much direction and purpose in Mr. C's discipline that he was ready to join the Marines.

But Joe's Navy veteran father promptly put an end to that idea with a blunt "Nope, you're not." Boggio Senior wanted his son to have the opportunity of college, so he offered up a deal. If Joe could pay for his first two years at community college, his parents would cover the last two years at Michigan State. So Joe lived at home. Flipped burgers at Wendy's. Made the 80-mile roundtrip drive each day to Kalamazoo Community College. He struggled at first. He'd gotten a D in algebra in high school, which wouldn't cut it for an aspiring engineer. But gradually, Joe built stronger study habits. His grades improved, and he applied to and was accepted at Michigan State. There he excelled in his classes, and had an epiphany: his engineering degree was reinforcing his natural tendency toward introversion. And so, during his junior year, Joe did something totally unexpected. He started a Toastmasters chapter at Michigan State. As he put it: "the exact opposite of my physiology."

Let's pause for a moment to let that sink in. A kid so fearful of people that he'd slinked away to an alternative school, yet rose up just a few years later to slay that inner dragon and advance past what Joseph Campbell would call his Threshold Guardian. Joe knew exactly what he had to do, and made a dramatic change in who he wanted to be. Nothing about this was easy. There was no one to guide him or hold his hand. Though he was nervous about starting his Toastmasters club, little by little it became "kind of exhilarating." And Joe didn't just lead Toastmasters, he started doing a lot of speaking and "getting into the routine of it, and it all started to feel really good."

As graduation neared, Joe took a decidedly proactive approach for a young man who'd once run from all manner of social interaction. He set an outlandish goal of doing 60 company interviews before he chose his career path. Joe wanted to master interviewing, to the point where he could "interview the interviewer," a dramatic role reversal for an extreme introvert. And with that radical objective in mind, he kicked into gear. He was anxious during the first handful of interviews. Then, pretty quickly, he became adept at anticipating the questions, and probing the true nature of each company. "The dynamic flipped," and Joe gained a deep understanding of the likely jobs he might get with his technical degree, and all of a sudden, the career of "a pure scientist engineer" looked awfully dull. Joe feared signing up for a spartan tech life with precious little human interaction, doomed to become "someone who would know more and more about less and less." Toastmasters and his forays into public speaking broadened his horizons, and taught him that instead of being down in the techie weeds he preferred "taking it up a level." He liked translating ideas and technology, and so he decided to accept a position in pre-sales at IBM. This might seem a small choice, shifting from the expected path of an engineer to pursuing technical sales. But Joe was staking out a different life where he would regularly engage and collaborate with others, one where he could be the master of his destiny. He might not be graduating from Stanford or about to launch a startup, but he had passed a critical hurdle. Joe was shifting into this new mindset so early in his life that for most people this would be the only Joe they'd ever know.

The Leader

Allan Finds His First Million

Allan walked into a Marine Corps office on Ocean Avenue in San Francisco. "Active duty or reservist?" the recruiter asked. His parents had tried to talk him out of it, but he hadn't forgotten the advice of that older gentleman he'd met while cutting class: "Study the leaders." Allan signed up to be a cook but scored too high on the entry exams. Instead, he was selected to work with satellite communications. That sounded great until he found out that he'd been tricked. The guys in SATCOM are sent to the front lines.

Allan was assigned to a Marine Corps company at Camp Pendleton in San Diego. Out of his 850 fellow recruits, he spotted perhaps five other Asian-Americans. He remembered the businessman's advice, and carefully observed the real leaders: the drill instructors, the captains, the officers. To Allan, "They seemed like superheroes. Their composure, their bearing."

Allan observed and made mental notes, and saw that the true leaders took care of their men. They wanted to be there, and they asked for and took responsibility. Allan saw this lesson borne out again and again during the arduous three months of boot camp. He "loved the training, the discipline, the principles," all the talk and lessons in "honor, courage, and commitment."

Drawn to the "physicality of everything" Allan focused intently on observing and learning from the brass. Allan tried to practice leadership himself, and soon earned the responsibility to lead a small squad. During the last week of boot camp, the company faced a brutal test — sleep and food deprivation, combined with the task of climbing a mountain with a heavy pack. They were given just two and a half days of food for the three days, and by the last day Allan had two meals left, and gave away one to his fellow recruits. The men liked Allan and he became one of the Honormen in the company, chosen to lead the final parade. But the military was not in his future. When his mother fell ill from tuberculosis, her son accepted an honorable discharge, and returned home to care for her for two years, taking her four times a week to San Francisco General for chemotherapy.

After his mother's recovery, Allan entered the College of San Mateo, joined the student government, and within a few weeks was elected student body president. "I wanted to practice leadership," he said. "How to organize people and show that I cared about them. How to be innovative." At the same time, he met his future wife. Both were accepted into UC Berkeley and BYU, and chose the latter and moved to Utah. Allan first took general education classes and then switched his major to philosophy "to learn to think right."

He was reading up on the tech industry, on the rebound after the recent dotcom crash. He began searching for a business or venture capital club, found one at the University of Utah, an hour away in Salt Lake City, and "ended up cutting school the first few weeks to spend time with them." The club members began cold-calling VC firms, volunteering to do research projects. Dozens said no. A few said yes, and their first projects were due diligence for technology venture funds. Allan researched music startups, voting startups, bio-tech, bioterrorism, Voice Over IP. He studied job boards for shifts in demand, sized up markets, gauged competition, and studied prior art patents.

"We ended up trying to start a fund," he said. "We pitched to all sorts of venture funds." Leaders don't ask for permission. They just do. It was crazy to expect these untested students to succeed in running a venture fund. "We didn't know what we were doing," Allan said. "We didn't know that we weren't supposed to do it."

Over the next few months Allan's group was rejected a hundred times. Then one notable VC who wished to remain anonymous wrote a personal check for $1 million. Buoyed by that investment, Allan pitched Merrill Lynch in Salt Lake and New York. Wells Fargo and Goldman Sachs made significant capital contributions.

And then there was Warren Buffett. Through a local connection, the team reached out to the Oracle of Omaha, and astonishingly were invited to visit – a remarkable opportunity to rub shoulders with a financial giant. The students flew out to Nebraska, and spent the better part of a day with Buffett. "He had more questions for us than we did for him," recalled Allan. "Our selection criteria. How we thought about tech investing." The visit would reinforce Allan's emergent thinking. "He had a barren, mundane office. It's all about simplicity and efficiency," said Allan. "The minimization of environmental noise. Designed so you can think in peace." And Allan admired the humble lifestyle Buffett lived despite being one of the world's richest men. That night he took them all to dinner at a steak house, and told them he'd enjoyed their visit and asked them to come back the following year.

Buffett did not invest. No matter. The group of college kids with no experience raised nearly $20 million. Mentored by a University of Utah business professor, along with several successful Utah-based business leaders, the student team scouted investments. "I was so excited," said Allan. "I started reading as much news as I could." He quickly discovered Omniture, a web analytics firm in nearby Provo, and spotted an opportunity. Omniture was one of the first companies to engineer a method to track people visiting ecommerce sites. Allan learned one of the founder's brothers was a classmate at BYU, and invited him to join their investment club.

All told, the students invested in 15 companies in Series A and B rounds, generally in $250,000 to $500,000 increments. Along the way, Allan and his fellow student venture capitalists gained tremendous experience while sitting in on their portfolio companies' board meetings as observers. Omniture, Allan's deal, went public in 2006, raising almost $70 million for a valuation of nearly $300 million. Four of the 15 companies went public, and the fund generated extraordinary returns for the investors. Allan Young, the former high school truant, had discovered what Jobs, Gates and many others had.

Sometimes it pays to skip class.

The Guardian

Karoli Takes a Sabbatical

Karoli came home from her high school year abroad in the U.S. and incorporated in Estonia. She sold 3,000 reflectors to a bus company, and 20,000 more to an insurance firm. She customized her reflector designs for clothing and jewelry, and demonstrated an intuitive grasp of marketing. She took meetings with car companies, and eventually Citroën gave her a free car for a year, an invaluable asset since her town was two hours from the capital. She followed up that coup by approaching a fuel company for free gas. "It took me only two meetings, so I basically got all the costs off the table." She had a free car and 200 complimentary liters of gas a month. Karoli sold reflectors in Estonia, Northern Europe and Portugal, winning more patents and international trademarks. Oh, and she did all this while earning her high school degree and graduating from college. "Basically, from six to 10 o'clock at night I was sitting in the university and during the day I was working on my company."

Karoli had a pulse on the youth market, and was a local success story. At 22, she got an offer to launch MTV in Estonia. Then, after a year, she caught the attention of the president of Fox Europe, who asked her to build up the Fox Entertainment channels in the Baltics, making her the youngest CEO in the company's history. The next three years, she worked through the worst of the global recession, while playing an instrumental role in making Fox the number one pay TV group in the Baltics. For almost anyone else, these would have been dream jobs. But Karoli was looking farther down the road. Already a proven force in media, with an open runway ahead, she abruptly left that industry behind and flew to Malaysia with her books and her running shoes for an overachieving millennial time out. "I thought, what am I going to do with my life?"

Island fever proved to be precisely what Karoli needed to kickstart the next phase of her career. Three weeks of relaxing in Malaysia convinced her even more thoroughly that she needed to dive into something radically different. Her Guardian instincts reinforced her need for a guiding purpose, "something to do besides running around on the island and reading books." She'd done traditional media. Maybe something in tech? Back in Estonia, she found a local media curation startup that needed a hand with its marketing efforts in the U.S. She flew 9,000 kilometers to Silicon Valley for her baptism-by-fire in the tech world, diving into pitching events, and immersing herself in the culture. She wasn't shy. She even cornered Dave McClure, Founder of the accelerator 500 Startups, spontaneously pitching him in a parking lot. He liked her energy, but not her startup, and sure enough he was right: the Estonian company tanked.

Karoli needed a new commitment, something that would change lives. She'd been hearing a lot about Singularity University, a renowned Silicon Valley accelerator with a mission to apply technology to tackling the world's most urgent environmental and social problems. Maybe one of Singularity's intensive programs would help her figure out what was next? By chance the admissions deadline was the very next day. Karoli rushed to fill out an application for the Graduate Studies Program, and crossed her fingers.

The Athlete

Joel Makes a List

The year was 2009. Joel had just landed a dream job, a marketing position with the Teva and Simple shoe lines of Deckers Brands in the beautiful coastal city of Santa Barbara, California. Six years after founding Untraditional, Joel had felt the global slowdown coming, and sold the Mountain Games to Vail, which later rebranded the event as the GoPro Mountain Games. Joel had not only successfully exited his first startup, he'd shifted effortlessly to what seemed a perfect transition for a guy with a wife and young family in search of stability.

The work was exciting. He was the Athlete, a man who'd helped to evangelize mountain and wilderness sports, and here he was working at the highest levels with a distinctly outdoor shoe brand. In two short years, Joel was promoted to President of Teva, a challenging role for a maverick marketer who'd never worked in the footwear business, and had never been on the payroll at a major company. Deckers was a publicly traded corporation with hundreds of millions of dollars in annual sales. Though the headquarters was in beautiful Santa Barbara, he'd left his mountain man lifestyle behind. No meetings on chairlifts, no days hunting powder or hiking the Rockies. For the first time in his life, Joel's day was dominated by desk time.

Joel slammed into his own personal pain point, and was surprised by how fast it happened. He was loving work, and putting in long hours at Teva. But exercise was taking a back seat, and then, suddenly, his whole body "started caving into itself." That first backache might have sent him to the doctor, or to gulp down pain pills. But the Athlete would have none of that. Instead, Joel experimented with a standing desk, then quickly realized that he'd simply shifted his sedentary state from his butt to his feet and knees. Now his hips hurt. Standing wasn't the silver bullet.

Everything was too stationary. Perhaps, thought Joel, even himself. At 40, with a growing family and a track record of entrepreneurial success, something totally unexpected hit him. Failure. The Teva brand had been struggling for a time, and it was a lot to expect this outdoorsman marketing entrepreneur from the Rockies to adapt to a publicly traded corporation, rife with the normal infighting. In late 2013 Joel had a particularly bad day at the office. His last day. "I was walked out," he said. "It wasn't my choice to leave Deckers by any stretch of the imagination." Joel saw himself as a turnaround guy and the job had become more operational. The why didn't really matter. Joel's seemingly promising corporate career was supposed to be predictable and secure. The anchor that he and his wife could count on for their future. And here he was on the street, dazed, not quite comprehending what had hit him.

After the initial shock passed, Joel went to the glass. He wasn't sure what was next, but he had what he thought were five great ideas. Some people scribble down business concepts in a notebook. Others on Post-its or a whiteboard. Joel penned his list on his bathroom mirror. He called it his shark tank. Five ideas staring back at him when he shaved in the morning. Five ideas that every day he moved a little further along.

Joel's wife didn't love having to share her mirror with his startup ideas. Why couldn't he be like everyone else? Get a job. Settle down. Do something normal. But she knew the man she loved and married would never be that guy. The mirror called. One of the concepts he kept coming back to was strikingly simple, one that he'd been pondering his last few corporate years, a balance board for the office, a novel approach to introduce movement into the static reality of so many workers' days, a fresh way to rebound from the pain he'd felt at being cooped up in the office, and perhaps, now that he'd been summarily banished, a rebel counterstrike against the corporate world that wouldn't have him.

The Conductor

Carlos Fights City Hall

On paper, Carlos's idea to create a food truck park seemed like an easy, straightforward project. U-Haul desperately wanted out of that drug-addict and rat-infested lot on 11th and Harrison in San Francisco. Carlos offered $6,000 a month to take over their $15,000 monthly lease, and the company gladly accepted the deal. But soon after signing the lease, he began to realize why no one had ever tried this before in the city. Carlos had assumed the permitting would be straightforward. The property was zoned SALI (Service, Arts, Light Industrial), widely considered the most laxly regulated category. What could be the problem? Carlos brought his plans to the planning department. No problem there. But then he had to pass through a bureaucratic maze. "You have go through all the desks: the fire department, the environmental department, the health department," he recalled. "They're literally desks, and everyone has a guideline."

When you break new ground as an entrepreneur there's no model. And there was certainly no guideline in San Francisco, the world's entrepreneurial epicenter, for the first food truck park. "So, at every single desk it was just a huge delay, a huge re-explanation of the project," said Carlos. "The process was horrible in every sense of the word." There was another personal issue. Carlos would accompany his contractor to each desk, and the bureaucrats would look askance at this 23-year-old trying to do something brand new. Half-ignoring Carlos's presence, they'd grumble to the contractor: "What does this kid want to do?"

Ten desks. Carlos's head spun. "One week you're at this desk, another week you're at the other desk. And when you change something with the fire guys it doesn't mean that coincides with what the environmental people want to see. So they'd say, 'Oh, why did the fire department tell you to do this? That doesn't work for us. Change it.'"

Carlos had imagined permitting would take just a few months. But half a year passed, with rent and architects' fees stacking up, the park yet to open. He hustled. He bought a prefab "barn" for $7,000 that he and his workers quickly assembled, that would provide covered seating for 70. He built bathrooms, brought in an old yellow school bus (which he somehow got for free) to serve as another hangout spot. He hooked up water and electrical, and dropped in some palms and plants, and "a million other things." A year after signing the lease, they finally raised the SoMa StrEat Food Park sign, just under the nearby freeway ramp. It was the spring of 2012. Word traveled fast. This was a genuinely new take on dining. Platforms were becoming all the rage in tech, and here was what sounded a lot like a food platform. *The San Francisco Chronicle*, CBS and the Huffington Post requested interviews, and a local TV station came and started filming while guys "were still sawing tables."

But the bureaucrats weren't done. San Francisco's Bureau of Street-Use and Mapping issued one final demand: Carlos had to plant 20 trees on the sidewalks circling the entire property. He had to cut and excavate the sidewalk, adding tens of thousands of dollars to the project. Add in the cost of the trees and planting, and the total bill would easily eclipse $70,000. Fighting City Hall isn't easy, even when you're an entrepreneur hoping to provide a valuable brand-new service. The enormous delays and costs of having to go through the labyrinth-like permitting process was taking its toll. Carlos considered throwing in the towel. Then took a deep breath.

"We're going to figure this out," he remembered saying. "We'll just make it happen." They started researching, and sure enough he discovered the Friends of the Urban Forestry, and sent out an SOS. Amazingly, the non-profit paid for nearly the whole job, trees and all. The weather was not cooperating. "They had about 20 people installing trees in the biggest downpour that year, and I was like, *Man, these people are just saving me, and I can't believe they are doing this right now.*"

Carlos got his trees planted. Finally, every last San Francisco desk was satisfied. But the toll of all the delays, cost overruns and setbacks was mounting. "It was a huge hit on my family," Carlos said. "There were fights, and it was scary." The young man couldn't sleep, worrying: *No one will come.* It had been a nutty idea, *my food truck farce.* Why hadn't he been satisfied with managing the family's established and safe restaurants? It was all his fault, and he knew it. His gamble was costing the family a small fortune.

This wasn't a game, or a college class project. A few days before SoMa StrEat Food Park's grand, scheduled opening, Carlos's heart began racing, and he couldn't stop it from beating like a machine gun, and he was rushed to the emergency room in the throes of a full-blown panic attack.

The Evangelist

Uwe Writes a New Script

Out in Bophuthatswana, Uwe Diegel was discovering the power of a hot product in a closed market. Africans couldn't get enough of his low-lactose milk tubes. "Every morning we had trucks coming in from the townships that would fill up with Fruity Flow, and they'd give us bundles of cash," he said. "It was the Wild West." Doubling in size each year, by year five they put the company up for sale. Nestle was interested, as Uwe's operation was selling more product locally than the Swiss conglomerate. Eight months of ploddingly slow due diligence later, Uwe was paid a surprise visit at the factory by a guy who arrived in a bulletproof BMW. Definitely not the Nestle rep. He was a Greek who ran all the local gambling dens. "I want your business," the Greek told Uwe. "How much do you want for it in cash?"

Tired of waiting for the Swiss, Uwe said Nestle's price was $2.5 million and he'd take less. The next day the Greek came with a suitcase filled with $2.4 million in cash. Recalled Uwe: "I know it sounds crazy but that's how we sold it."

Flush with success, Uwe was ready to do it again. That's when his father-in-law brought back a digital thermometer from Taiwan. "My cousin invented this," he told Uwe. "What do you think we can do with it?" Uwe had never considered selling healthcare instruments, but the idea grabbed him, so he registered a company, then flew to Taiwan and asked a score of Taiwanese manufacturers for the right to distribute their products in South Africa. And just like that, Uwe was soon importing all kinds of pseudo-medical devices. He developed a nose for what might sell, a knack for marketing. He'd quickly shifted from a concert pianist to a guy with a food factory, and then to a guy constantly looking for the next hot gadget. "I spent a lot of time going to the Hong Kong Fair, the Shenzhen Fair, the Taipei Fair," he said. "I'd find a gizmo that I thought would be cool and then I would say, how can I sell it?"

Fifteen products down the line, he was growing weary of the ephemeral nature of the business. After a couple of years, he said to himself: *I'm tired of constantly looking for the next gadget. What I need to do is build a brand, build a story.* Uwe needed a team, and hooked up with a Norwegian ex-pat, Morten Brunvoll, and three other partners. They hatched the concept for a full-fledged, comprehensive medical brand. The head office had to be in Switzerland because you gain instant credibility when "you put that little Swiss flag with Swiss accuracy, and all that." Six months later they were selling digital thermometers in beautiful packages from their new company, Microlife, for double the price of competing products from China. There was one problem. Mercury thermometers were still cheaper. He needed a compelling story to drive the brand. And so in 1994, Uwe launched the Microlife international mercury recuperation campaign. "I just thought it was a cool thing to do," he said. "I knew how dangerous mercury thermometers were. So, I said, 'Let's see if we can ban them.'" Uwe wrote articles about tragic cases of mercury poisoning and toxic levels of the element in the Great Lakes. He became the face of the worldwide anti-mercury proliferation campaign.

Four years later, in November of 1998, the French government banned mercury thermometers, soon to be followed by dozens of other countries and the entire European Union. "It just turned out at that moment I happened to manufacture 67 percent of the worldwide production of non-mercury thermometers," said Uwe. "That was quite interesting. It taught me the whole thing about planting seeds. Not just planting seeds but watering them as you went along, to make long-term products."

The Visionary
Risto Thinks Big by Going Small

Pain inspired Risto. The pain of a world full of so many lousy digital products. "I was already frustrated by all the crappy stuff. IBM had Notes, Microsoft came out with their shit. It was frustrating. It looked bad. It didn't serve any purpose in any real way," he recalled. "Remember how nobody could program their VHS recorder? I was like, *it can't be that hard.* My dad, he's a smart guy. My mom, she's smart, but they were not able to use it, and they paid their month's salary to buy one." That was the impetus. That foundational friction Risto felt between man and machine. "The idea came: 'Can we somehow help companies create products that would actually be intuitive and easy to use?'"

Risto needed to connect that pain with a business insight. He found that connection doing deep focus group analyses while producing expensive ad campaigns for Finland's biggest newspapers. He became skilled in a more fluid method of user research. Risto could zero in on people's values, attitudes, and crucial patterns of behaviors. He began to know precisely how to design for them. That discovery led Risto to found Oujee, and lead dozens of international user research projects, including major global explorations for then-booming Nokia. "We turned our usability analysis and user research reports into inspirations for designs," he said. "This is how it should look. This is how it should feel."

One afternoon Risto doodled in his notebook, playing with the word "Idea." He liked how it looked. He added an "n" to the end and liked it even more. In Finnish, Idean meant, *I've got an idea*, which plugged right into his company's emerging ethos. That doodle led to Idean Research and Idean Creative. But this major shift in identity was controversial. Usability research was defined, predictable, profitable – his sacred cow. Design was ambiguous, uncharted. Risto's co-founders and advisors saw risk. Shouldn't Idean do one or the other? "We even had internal fights, like, 'Well, we know user research. How can we be designers?'" recalled Risto. "I was like, 'That's the only fucking thing I want to be!'"

Risto saw their pioneering research methodology as a primary tool for a modern digital designer, ideal inspiration for great digital design. They might have been 9,000 kilometers from Silicon Valley, but Idean was on the front line of a lot of new user-centered principles and methods, part of a momentous time. "It's like 1969, when everyone was at Woodstock, and it became a movement," he said. "We just happened to be in Helsinki, and we had some really cool projects."

Risto bet the farm on design. In a single year he hired at least a dozen designers "in a field where there were no designers." He hunted down skilled art directors and traditional designers, and trained them for this burgeoning realm of digital screens. To his mind his designers quickly became among the world's best at what soon became known as interaction design, and later UX design. "We were digital native. From day one, it's been all about the human-centric digital stuff."

Idean was doing intriguing projects for Nokia, the world's leading mobile phone juggernaut. It was frustrating at times because a good chunk of what they created never saw the light of day, an early sign of the corporate paralysis that would doom Nokia. But like a handful of other digital design consultancies around the world, Risto sensed a seismic shift underway. The Visionary saw what was coming. "This is hard to explain, but we were in a business, like the IDEOs or the Frog Designs where we were seeing three years from now, and even farther away. What I'm saying is that a lot of the designers at Idean, they also saw it. They were able to dream it."

The iconic platform for the screen-centric smartphone world Risto wanted to build his company around? Steve Jobs's iPhone.

The Accidental

Mait's French Connection

Mait really, really wanted to learn French. He hypothesized that he could tap vast oceans of data – verbal particles, patches of real conversational language – to unlock all kinds of patterns in the learning process, and had a hunch that movies might hold the key to developing fluency. "I wanted to learn the conversation," he recalled. "The one you have in real life." Mait was a physicist with some tremendous resources at his disposal. He thought big, very big. He wrote a small program and started vacuuming up movies into CERN's supercomputers, crawling movie databases and download-ing the text files of movie subtitles in French. This was a mountain of data, to the tune of 50,000 movies. Mait wrote algorithms to sift through the files to identify the key words that make up the bulk of spoken French, the words that matter.

As he began fashioning his prototype, Mait also wanted to quantify his own memory, so he "put together the mathematics to make it more optimal," to pace and design language labs in the way that our short-term and long-term memory actually work. This iterative process continued for more than six months, an elaborate experiment with a specific goal. Mait spent two hundred hours studying with his supercomputer-inspired, data-rich program, then took the high school graduation test in French, and to his "surprise, passed it with an above average result." His personal success validated his theory. Though he was lousy at languages, if he studied the right words, in the right way for his memory and style of learning, he could dramatically accelerate his fluency.

Just as particles collided in the Hadron accelerator in unpredictable ways, Mait then happened to run into Jaan Tallinn, one of the co-founders of Skype, an Estonian startup legend and heralded investor. Jaan had also trained at the University of Tartu in the very same discipline of theoretical physics. The two met at a physics conference in Estonia and quickly discovered that by chance they were both taking a technical deep dive into the learning of languages, writing their own custom computer programs. Jaan invited the young physicist to his home. "We really looked into the details," said Mait. "How the code is written, the algorithms." Creating a French language learning model was an accident. So too was this serendipitous meeting of mind and code. Jaan had written a program to learn Japanese, in part because he had no prior knowledge of the tricky language. "We spent half a day looking at each other's code," said Mait. "The networks, the neural networks." Jaan was impressed, and informed Mait that his program was so much better than his own, that "OK, you have to start a company."

Mait didn't consider Jaan's suggestion a real option. He was a serious scientist with a PhD in theoretical physics and an already distinguished body of work. The French experiment had been a hobby. The Accidental was not planning to abandon his career. Sure, Mait thought, somebody could make this language learning program, but it wasn't going to be him. He thanked Jaan for an enjoyable afternoon, and went back to his job as a physicist at CERN.

Takeaways:
Shifting into Gear

Getting started. Moving from talking and dreaming to actually doing. The Faces provide distinct approaches for how to take action. Who helps you get down to business?

Makers seek product validation, not outside approval.
Collaborators experiment by trying on new personas.
Leaders sign up for opportunities to lead.
Outsiders boldly crash other worlds.
Athletes commit to training regimes.
Visionaries go big by tightening their focus.
Evangelists plant seeds for tomorrow's growth.
Conductors forge harmonies from dissonance.
Guardians look past early success for a nobler goal.
Accidentals go deep with their passion projects.

The Place

Mait knew that if they walked away from their conversation that day, thinking they'd pick it up again in a week or two, "then probably we would have just had a nice discussion" and nothing would happen. But Estonia is arguably the world's most digitally advanced nation. You can register a new business in a minute. Ott exclaimed, "OK, let's start doing it!" and he pulled up the government site on his smartphone and registered their company.

We call it The Place. The ecosystem. The city pulsing with tremendous networking opportunities. The right university, accelerator, or social network. The nurturing environment that serves up just what it takes. What makes the place hum is more than institutions and buildings. Mindset is paramount. Ambitious talent, business savvy, technical talent, and a healthy tolerance for risk. Entrepreneurs and investors who've already succeeded, still hungry for another run at the mountain. You hear it on the street. Feel it in the meetups. Share it in the cafés: a burning need to make. Collaborate. Create.

The next point is hard to convey and harder to grasp. Only you can make the most of your Place. And while you can seek out that perfect formula in a nation, city or university, what you create depends on how you show up. This is a soup of your own making, and you must often not only add the vegetables but the spice.

Place can be virtual. A distributed digital community, a professional network, a platform with access to peers and experts with complementary skills. The pandemic made remote collaboration an absolute necessity. Workshops and events instantly went totally online. Teams bonded over distance, and new voices and leaders emerged in this 100 percent digital medium. Those who quickly adopted these new skills at creating and collaborating online had an edge.

Whether a virtual or physical Place, you've got choices. You can plug into an established ecosystem or take the exciting, independent path of building one yourself. Plugging in offers the security of context and connections. Building your own gives you a chance to become a leader of your own movement. Either way, Place is paramount. Zero in on the right city, with the right resources, people, programs, and mojo, and you just might make it to the next stage. For in nearly every case, you must come to grips with this harsh reality. No matter how brightly you burn in your desire to create something original and powerful, you have to make your own luck, starting with putting yourself where serendipity is most likely to strike.

The Maker

Perry Comes Home

A s Perry struggled to sell two or three snowshoes at a time to small, independent stores, the scope of the challenge dawned on him. He was a traveling salesman with a one-off product. Perry's design was a true breakthrough, weighing three or four pounds instead of ten, made out of aluminum and nylon instead of wood and rawhide. But the world was not beating a path to his innovation. There wasn't a snowshoeing magazine or a snowshoe club, and certainly no tribe of enthusiasts. That's often one of the hardest lessons for the aspiring entrepreneur. Products rarely sell themselves. Perry had to reinvent the experience of snowshoeing.

What he didn't realize at the time was that he would draw on all sorts of lessons from Dennis Boyle's Design Garage class and his training under David Kelley. True, Perry was well on his way to designing and building a great snowshoe, soon applying for and receiving the first new patents in snowshoes in 43 years. But the pastime itself was moribund and solitary, a broken experience. Products don't sell in a vacuum, and quite simply people didn't know where they could snowshoe. In most mountain areas, you had to buy a permit to park and snowshoe. The robust network of ski resorts and snowboard parks so integral to the massive popularity of those winter sports was strikingly absent from snowshoeing. Perry would have to look to other sports for inspiration.

Seeing the running craze take off in California, Perry teamed up with Nike to organize snowshoe races. The Maker was prototyping a novel snowshoe experience. "People would snowshoe from the bottom to the top of the mountain," he said. "We thought this was it. We'd do these big races." The competitions didn't generate sales, but the efforts attracted attention. Perry met Jerry Greenfield of Ben and Jerry's Ice Cream, a snowshoe aficionado and an inspiration for a new wave of "full moon snowshoe and ice cream walks" at major ski resorts. Atlas became Vail's "official" snowshoe provider. Perry loaded up his Blazer again, and hit the trade show circuit, and made inroads with REI, the Seattle-based outdoor retailer.

But to truly break through Perry had to make something bigger. He took a risk and kicked in $80,000 to sponsor Beaver Creek to put in a snowshoe trail. Ski Area Management Magazine wrote a cover story. "It was: boom! Vail, Intrawest, Whistler, Blackcomb, all of the top ten ski resorts, we got them to put in snowshoe parks," said Perry. "It was amazing. It put the halo of credibility of usage into snowshoeing." Perry had created a full-fledged snowshoeing ecosystem, rapidly gaining traction with the public.

Atlas's sales jumped from $200,000 in 1992 to $1 million in 1993, doubling in 1994, and doubling yet again to $4 million in 1995. For the modest business of snowshoes, this was achieving scale in a few short years. Perry Klebahn had done it. Starting in Stanford's Design Garage, he had spied an opportunity, created a product, and most importantly built out a comprehensive experience, and an industry. In late 1999, with annual sales of $10 million, he sold Atlas Snowshoes to a competitor. Great. But now what? Perry had successfully created a sophisticated product ecosystem. Where would he thrive next? What would be his personal ecosystem, his new Place?

David Kelley wanted Perry Klebahn to come back to Stanford, to teach the very class in which he had found the spark for his startup. But Perry was itching to experience the corporate world. Two months after selling Atlas, he took on a new job at the legendary outdoor gear maker Patagonia, in Ventura, California.

But he would find it hard to resist Kelley and Stanford. The IDEO founder soon talked him into teaching a spring class while he worked at Patagonia. Then, after five amazing years at Patagonia, Perry was courted for a CEO position in San Francisco. Before starting at Timbuk2, he took a Stanford sabbatical, teaching full time that spring. It was only a matter of time. He'd caught the teaching bug.

The Shift that swung him fully back into Stanford's orbit came when Kelley included Perry among a talented group of professors he tasked with creating something radical. Kelley thought holistically. This was about expanding his method beyond engineering and traditional industrial design. Imagining a whole new ecosystem on campus. But at Stanford a program needed to die before a new one could take possession of an existing facility. "It's funny," recalled Perry. "I remember David saying, 'The bad news and good news is that we've got the shittiest location on campus.'" Kelley had sofas moved into a trailer and brought in a mix of top faculty and younger talent to hash out what this thing was going to become. Perry's teaching peers were Stanford management professor and IDEO fellow Bob Sutton, Chris Flink, another top IDEO veteran, the creativity guru Tina Seelig — all major players in business innovation. The trailer was a physical metaphor for the radical, empathy-centric, free-flowing, learn-from-your-mistakes cross-disciplinary program Kelley hoped to inspire. "If you can spill a can of paint on the floor and you don't care," Kelley told the group, "That's what we need right now!"

Kelley was a master at putting up a big tent, bringing in talent, and making stuff happen. That fall, Stanford announced that thanks to a $35-million donation from the SAP co-founder, Stanford's School of Engineering had launched the Hasso Plattner Institute of Design on campus, the realization of Kelley's lifelong "dream to bring faculty and students from different departments together to tackle interesting needs and innovation." The public quickly came to know it as the d.school, a model soon imitated around the world. Perry would teach many classes, but his favorite would come in 2009 when he quit corporate life, and returned to the campus for good.

Perry brainstormed with one of his favorite teaching partners. Michael Dearing had superb credentials, a bachelor's in economics from Brown, a Harvard MBA, and a long profitable executive run at eBay. Now he was turning his cash and knowledge into becoming one of Silicon Valley's elite angel investors. The two men pondered.

What if they led a class where everybody wanted to start something? Where the class was not required? Where it was all about starting up? They were the perfect team. Perry knew how to drive students to prototype ruthlessly, to push for sales early on. Michael was a true technology industry veteran. "He knew about tech stuff," said Perry. "He was fearless to start. Michael was like, 'Yeah, fuck it, let's do it. Let's go!'"

They had a name for the new Place. They called it Stanford Launchpad.

The Outsider
Daniel Opens a New Door

A single fish in a giant school is both an individual and a part of the whole, and at Stanford, Daniel Lewis was swimming in rich, nutrient-dense waters in concert with many others. The campus was the perfect intersection of place, people and resources: a healthy habitat for growth. Opportunities that presented themselves organically were part of why Stanford was such a tremendous global engine for entrepreneurship – this was, after all, where the legends of tech had played and hacked and built giant companies. Daniel swam better than most because he was attuned to that culture and took advantage of its benefits. He never planned on a startup. "The legal tech thing was just a hobby originally," recalled Daniel. "Kind of a creative outlet to do something. And I just found myself spending more and more nights and weekends on it. Enjoying the process."

It was uncanny how one thing led to the next at Stanford. Daniel's hobby was becoming so much more, aided by a year of extensive, creative research, the venture capital course, and their snowballing success in the university's business plan competition. By spring Daniel and Nik were most definitely onto something. They progressed through the early business plan competition rounds, gaining confidence with each pitch. It was an ideal platform for a couple of law students – writing a sober, well-defined plan and presenting before a panel of judges.

Launchpad was another skillset entirely. A big stretch. But they were diligent. They kept coming back week after week and clearly demonstrated to the professors that they were a solid team. This was Launchpad's third year, and by then Perry Klebahn figured they'd vetted more than a couple hundred founders during office hours. Launchpad too had to act like a startup. Take risks. Not fall into the rut of prejudging who should or should not be admitted. And Perry had already learned the value of taking fliers on teams outside the normal range. Like a couple of law students. "We were just like, "This is amazing," Perry recalled. "Let's find a way to get them in the class."

Daniel and Nik overcame the first hurdle the professors put in front of them, the requirement that they talk with fellow law students about their concept, and create a crude paper prototype. They began sketching mock-ups of "what the first few screens of this website would look like." They lacked design skills, but hustled, getting their sketches into a rapid wireframing tool called Balsamiq. After that encouraging first step, Perry and Michael bore down on them, prodding them to engage in quick, focused experiments. And that's where the law school students floundered. Their legal search concept sounded fabulous. Yes, they had cool visual bubble chart graphics to show the relative significance of different precedents. But the rookies had what might be called entrepreneur's block. The obstacle: their cautious mindset. They were firmly convinced they couldn't go any further until they somehow got their hands on a massive database of legal precedents. They'd clearly need an expensive partnership with a law library. Attorneys wouldn't trust anything else. "We simply must get content," Daniel asserted. "It has to be real." Little did they know that this line of stubborn thinking and "non-doing" might be called Prototyping Fallacy #101.

The professors responded to that mental roadblock with a textbook lesson on what they called *the stage of decoupling assumptions.*

"Tell me why you put those two things together?" asked Michael.

"Well, an attorney has to have real information."

"No, no," Michael pushed back. "No, I got that. Let's say an attorney gets real information on a case. Why does that mean you have to have a partnership with a law library?"

"Well, we have to get the content from somebody."

"Yeah, you need to get content for the one prototype. That

doesn't equal a partnership with a law library. It equals content for a single case."

The professor let that sink in for Daniel and Nik, for everyone. "What are the many ways we could brainstorm getting content for one case?"

The Accidental

Mait Enters Tallinn's Orbit

Pundits rave about the giant tech hubs — San Francisco, London, Berlin, Paris. But it's not about size. It's about Place, concentration, and how tightly woven is your network. And there's the other impetus that a robust ecosystem can deliver in a pinch. The timely push we often need to move from dreaming and contemplating to doing.

There is no certainty that anyone tips over to the life of an entrepreneur, and as a man who knew his quantum mechanics and Heisenberg's uncertainty principle, Mait Müntel knew that forward momentum, whether for a particle or a human being, could not be precisely determined. Mait, for instance, appeared to be continuing on his regular orbit. Like clockwork, he returned to CERN, resumed life as a brilliant physicist, and might have continued along that path and forgotten all about his language-learning program were it not for a chance encounter. Six months had passed since Jaan Tallinn had told him to start a company, and predictably nothing much had happened. This, of course, was in tune with Newton's first law of physics, the principle of inertia, that "a body with no net force acting on it will either remain at rest or continue to move with uniform speed in a straight line."

Mait was attending an alumni event at the University of Tartu in Estonia when he ran into Ott Jalakas, an old schoolmate. "We knew that we existed, but we were not big friends before." Ott was a successful businessman who, like a lot of enterprising Estonians, had worked internationally. Ott had been head of strategy with Swedbank, and had taken extended research trips to Ukraine, Vietnam and Belgium. "He knew the pain of living in another country without knowing the language," said Mait. "And how great it would be to learn quickly. So the idea triggered his imagination."

They agreed to meet the following day, whereupon Ott did something ambitious Estonians do every day, because entrepreneurism is in the air there, because the tiny nation in the shadow of Russia is always thinking global. Mait knew that if they walked away from their conversation that day, thinking they'd pick it up again in a week or two, "then probably we would have just had a nice discussion" and nothing would happen. But Estonia is arguably the world's most digitally advanced nation. You can register a new business in a minute. "OK, let's start doing it!" Ott exclaimed, and he pulled up the government site on his smartphone and registered their company.

That timely shove from the seasoned businessman pushed Mait past another threshold. The logical scientist in him began calculating what would be next. Sure, he'd hacked out some software, but he wasn't a true software developer. His language learning program had no front-end: "It was not nice, it didn't have any design, and it was super complicated to install on anybody's computer." They needed someone to write clean code. Ott, the businessman, thought it would be wise to do this the traditional way, to pay for professionals, and so they applied for and got a €15,000 bank loan backed up with their homes. This was another layer of commitment. Mait wrote his first product spec, and they contracted with two different companies, one to write the front-end, and the other to write the back-end. Mait, being a rookie, learned too late this was not a good idea: "I got two pieces which were not working together."

The €15,000 had been spent, with nothing useful to show for it. Mait had taken a vacation from CERN with the expectation that he could direct this early product development and then return to Switzerland and manage it from afar. Now they needed to hire more programmers, and Mait realized he had to extend his vacation – and get more money fast. They had to hustle, and got lucky, finding a young and green developer at the university "who didn't know anything about how much developers make." Considering they had very little cash it was a perfect match. The young coder quickly managed to get the front and back ends to connect. "He developed a lot of new stuff superfast," said Mait. "Without having any experience, and without us having any experience in giving him clear instructions." This again was part of the secret of Estonia's success. Gifted young talent willing to dive into a tricky technical project.

But they were out of funds and needed more technical help. Mait paid a visit to Jaan Tallinn, and launched into a story that very much fit the Accidental. "It seems we have founded a company," he told the man who played a central role in creating the $8 billion global success known as Skype. "It was not planned," Mait told him sheepishly. "But now we have a company. We have a developer." Jaan listened patiently and gave Mait some advice on what to do next. And then it suddenly dawned on Mait that this had been an investment meeting. By the time he walked out, Jaan Tallinn had kicked in €50,000, essential capital to keep the dream alive. Mait and Ott hired a couple more developers, and Mait soon realized that writing complex software took a lot longer than he had anticipated. The summer dragged on, the code was still unfinished, and he had to extend his vacation from CERN once again, until finally in August he realized there was no going back.

The Guardian
Karoli Finds Her Singularity

Sitting in classes at Singularity University Karoli found herself surrounded by "amazing people talking about where technologies are headed and how they will transform the lives of billions." She heard how drones would soon be delivering medicines to remote regions, how food would be modified to save children from malnutrition. Another woman might have wondered if she belonged. But Karoli found herself in a place and a stage of her life where she was even more inclined to think long-term. There was another reason she was eager to find what might be next. Pregnant with her first child, she knew that she'd want to spend some time with her daughter after her birth. She was searching for something meaningful to work on for the long term. She needed her big idea, that larger purpose. Before class, in the mornings, her favorite running route happened to be next to the Google campus, and as she trotted by the buildings, she wondered. *Why are the great tech companies concentrated here? Why are so many things happening here in this place?*

Karoli realized that it wasn't about brains. The people in Silicon Valley weren't that much smarter than those in other countries. Over the years, the region had simply become a gathering point for the top firms and brightest talent, developing an overwhelming gravitational pull. The Guardian in her considered if she could mimic that effect in other cities, mulling over the germ of an idea, one unlikely to come from say a highly advantaged (and perhaps at times myopic) native San Franciscan. "So I started to think, what if we distribute those knowledgeable people to places that don't necessarily have that knowledge?"

Singularity was about more than just fascinating lectures and readings. Students had to pitch a project, attract a team and take it to the next level. Karoli pitched her nascent international work concept. She'd roughed out an idea for a platform to help make it easier for people to find work and immerse themselves in other cultures, while simultaneously supporting companies to source international talent. And then something totally unexpected happened. This young woman who'd been chosen to lead when she was sixteen, this talent who had embraced leadership naturally, was confronted with a very unfamiliar response: "I didn't get followers," she said. "Everybody wanted to do robots or something more exciting." Karoli was flummoxed. She'd had so few setbacks in her life. Failing to gain traction, she joined another Singularity squad and began working on someone else's idea. For another young professional, that rejection might have been taken as a sign from the universe. Go back to working in TV. Let go of the dream. Perhaps, after all, it was a bit presumptuous to think a tech neophyte from tiny Estonia could revamp global work. She returned home, never quite forgetting that dream of inclusion and opportunity that hit her during that morning run by Google's campus.

The Visionary

Risto Takes a Walk Down University Avenue

Risto Lähdesmäki was walking down Palo Alto's charming tree-lined University Avenue when the thought hit him like a warm breeze. "I didn't even know what Palo Alto really was. I had no clue, but I fell in love with that street. I had this feeling inside me that this is my home." The feeling was tied to the vibe of the street and town, the extended Stanford sphere of influence, and the potential he felt for his company. The Visionary trusted his instinct, followed his gut. Risto had the feeling a couple of times before, and every time he'd trusted it. He lived in Helsinki, halfway around world, but in that instant, he thought to himself: *This is my place.*

The last few years had been a roller coaster. Though he'd steadily built up his company's sales, Risto had learned the hard way that ignoring his instincts could be dangerous. He'd listened to traditional wisdom and hired a professional CEO. At the same time, Idean had made a big bet on China, and he flew there regularly to drum up business. It all felt off to Risto, and eventually he realized he'd taken advice from the wrong people. The CEO clashed with their free-spirited culture, and had to be let go, a setback that proved costly as a poorly drafted shareholder agreement gave early hires outsized control. Chinese firms, meanwhile, had yet to recognize the value of high-end UX design, and Risto lost a million dollars and valuable time trying to change their thinking.

It all came to a skidding halt at summer's end in 2008 with the global economic meltdown. Suddenly, Risto had to halve his staff from 60 to 30. He buckled down and split his time between sales and design, taking a lean approach. Business gradually improved. "We did tiny projects, $10,000 to $20,000 on average, but that trained us to become super-efficient. Traveling regularly for sales pitches, Risto became more confident that he could scale and go global, that being from tiny Finland could be a strategic advantage. "Our Scandinavian heritage: minimalist and to the point. We had clients saying, 'Yeah, it makes total sense to hire a Finnish design agency.'"

Proud of his nation's white and blue flag, Risto dreamed of planting it somewhere bold. The Visionary instinctively knew that he needed a more inspiring place. But his board took pains to remind him of his recent management disasters. Risto was also bumping up against his hometown constraints. Finland in 2010 was still defined by its socialist foundations. "You either work for Nokia or you're a teacher, doctor, or priest," said Risto. "Those are your four options. Being an entrepreneur is like, *Well, we can try once. You will fail, and when you fail you'll become a Nokia employee.* I hated that."

In 2010 Risto had a serious chat with Ossi Pohjola, the chairman of his board, a man he considered a second father. Risto shared his plan to take Idean to the San Francisco Bay Area. Ossi looked him in the eye, and said: 'Dude, don't you remember what just happened?'" It seemed a sensible note of caution. No one had made the leap before from Finland. Nor was the chairman alone in his thinking. Practically everyone Risto talked to said it was impossible. But he had already bought his ticket, and told them simply, "I'll be away for a while."

Risto landed his first California deal during that initial two-week Palo Alto exploratory trip in January of 2011. He returned home with the purchase order, and jetted back two weeks later and made another sale. He settled on a rhythm of two weeks in Palo Alto, two weeks in Helsinki, always staying at the Sheraton in Palo Alto, his new California home. Risto practiced minimalist communiques to the home office. No phone calls. No narratives. Just simple emails – with purchase orders attached.

Skilled designers are great at prototyping or testing just about anything. Risto was testing whether he could move Idean to Silicon Valley's heartbeat. Now, when he met potential clients and contacts Risto was a local, "just traveling a lot in Europe." He knew that if potential Bay Area clients saw him as yet another visiting or temporary foreign wannabe he wouldn't be taken seriously. After a few successful Palo Alto trips, he began to think his dream might come true. "What I learned was that finally there was a budget line on Excel, which said user experience design. I didn't need to preach anymore. Every single CEO, let's say nine out of ten, would know why experience is important in software and why that added value. Whereas in Finland and Europe, that number would be one out of ten."

Risto was a man who believed courage and belief were intertwined, a fire that needed to be stoked. He set himself another tough goal: to find one client who didn't come from any friends or pre-existing clients. "Just a pure, local company." He wanted to do such an amazing job for that company that it would refer Idean to friends without asking. Risto met the founders of the nearby tech startup Sentilla, and said he'd only charge them $8,000 for a two-day UX design workshop, far below the going rate. This was Risto planting a seed. Sentilla was a hot, venture-backed startup doing complex IT infrastructure software. This was part of his gamble. Take a chance with some startups, because you'd never know. One might turn into the next Instagram.

Risto had the creativity, foresight and chutzpah to understand that shifting his center of gravity to Palo Alto would move the needle. He was jetting toward the biggest base of UX customers in the world. That year, the Finn would spend more than a hundred nights at the Sheraton in Palo Alto, until the staff called him Risto, and he really was living nearly half his life in California. The dream was becoming reality, one trip and one deal at a time. All on a gut feeling. Now all Risto had to do was to truly make Palo Alto his place.

The Athlete
Joel Sets Up Shop

J oel Heath did not have the luxury of attending Stanford University or of living in the red-hot Bay Area. He had just lost his job, and was hardly in the epicenter, 300 miles down the coast in laid-back Santa Barbara. This might have seemed to be a terrible position in which to be bold, except that it was strikingly close to the origin story of a great many entrepreneurs when they first dipped their toes in the water. Not unlike, for instance, James Dyson, who first toyed with his multibillion-dollar vacuum cleaner idea while out of work.

Joel had five ideas on his bathroom mirror. No job, no income, no concept of what might be next. While it might have seemed prudent to take on some part-time work or consulting in the wake of his abrupt departure from Teva, his gut told him that would be a mistake.

Joel was an Athlete, training for the race of his life. He had to be all in.

Entrepreneurs often settle into the rich environment of a top-flight university, hip incubator or accelerator. Joel got his start in more auspicious surroundings, the same humble spot where a good chunk of new businesses launch: the family home. The Heath cottage, to be exact. Joel had built it in the backyard originally as a place to escape after the birth of his second son. There was a workspace for him, a yoga studio for his wife, a bed for overnight guests. Now the cottage became ground zero for Joel's second startup. His Place.

He moved in a standing desk, and soon discovered that his balance board idea was topping his list. Time to start tinkering, experimenting with form and function. The startup moved to the garage. A talent for wood carving ran in the family. His great grandmother and grandfather had both been talented wood carvers. Joel had inherited their classic tools, and now began using them to fashion his first primitive balance boards.

Yet for all the Silicon Valley mythology about the value of launching a business in a garage, Joel found, as so many budding entrepreneurs do, that launching a business in the family's living space was anything but romantic. He soon began spending part of his day at a nearby Santa Barbara co-working space. That got him out of the house, but the environment struck him as sterile, and there was a pretty big disconnect. Joel was sitting in a traditional desk chair because he didn't dare let strangers see what he was cooking up.

Despite these ordinary surroundings, Joel had been actively plugging into his local network, a world that had little to do with his cottage, garage or co-working space. He was diving into a startup that in business school terms would be called a classic adjacency. On the surface it appeared that Joel knew nothing about designing a balance board for the office, but by chance he had developed a robust network. The last few years at Teva's parent company Deckers Joel had worked with experts in footwear, movement, design and manufacturing. They might not know balance boards, but boy did they know reams about how movement affects your feet, your legs, your body. Santa Barbara – steeped in footwear, obsessed with surfing, surrounded by leading lifestyle companies – was the perfect Place to shake up the traditional limitations of the office environment.

Joel rallied a core group, starting with Kurtis Sakai, a contract footwear designer he'd worked with at Deckers. They surfed, talked, and ideated, and Joel soon hired him to sketch initial drawings. There was also an ex-pat with manufacturing experience in China whom Joel invited over. Sitting in Joel's backyard, the expert questioned why he wouldn't want to keep production close at home, a suggestion which dramatically shifted Joel's thinking. Over coffee with Jonas Brickus, his former creative director at Teva, Joel was matched up with a talented designer who by chance had just moved to town from New York.

The idea on the mirror was taking shape.

The Leader

Allan Discovers Seth Godin's altMBA

Allan Young was restless for his next Place. He dropped out of college, co-founded his first company, and built social networking tools, Flash widgets and embedded video. Then quickly shifted to ad tech. Allan was studying tech on his own terms. He joined his first startup, MediaForge, attracting interest and an initial $1.5 million in funding from the giant Japanese e-commerce firm Rakuten. The former philosophy major improvised, chasing a different sort of knowledge and experience. Wanting to work with his hands, he put in a six-month stint with an industrial design firm, designing mobile phone accessories, when gradually it dawned on him that he was missing something critical.

Allan had never taken a single business or economics class, and then out of thin air, an unusual program appeared – led by an unusual man. "There's this amazing guy named Seth Godin," a friend told him. "He wants to do this alternative MBA program." The name didn't register. Allan had never heard of him, but Godin already was a force with a growing, massive web following, a bestselling author and marketing guru. Allan looked Godin up and saw that he was an expert in marketing. "I had this wonderful experience with venture capital, I helped launch a startup, and I hadn't taken a business class before. I thought maybe the area of business I wanted to learn was marketing."

Forty-eight thousand people visited Godin's page announcing his altMBA. Three hundred and fifty applied. Allan was one of 27 whom Godin picked and invited to a beautiful apartment converted into a comfortable office in Hastings-on-Hudson in upstate New York. Godin told them to meet as many people as possible, and... disappeared. Ever mysterious, Godin had made a name for himself by his contrarian ideas. A couple of hours later the enigmatic leader returned and asked them to write down, "Who would you most like to be in the program with?" After they left, Godin tallied up the results. Nine or ten names kept coming up. Godin had cleverly crowd-sourced the selection. On January 20, 2009, he wrote: "the most selective (one in 40 got in) MBA program in the world got started."

Allan and eight other talented individuals became the first cohort of Seth Godin's altMBA. This was a major decision. It required that Allan move with his wife from Utah to Manhattan. But it fit right in with the concept of a Leader in search of knowledge. Here was another remarkable opportunity to get close to a maverick figure in business. "I was coming off my first start up, and I had invested in another startup and joined them to work for a little while," said Allan. "I just left and said, 'Yeah, let's try this, let's give it a shot.'"

From the start it was unconventional. The program didn't cost anything, and "Seth cooked lunch for us every day," recalled Allan. "That was the first, 'Holy shit, what is this? This guy is kind of different.'" They read dozens of books, including Godin's hit *Purple Cow*. The author delivered MBA-style lessons in his living room. "We put together four long conference tables to form a big square and we sat around that square. We would be on one side and he would be on the other, and he'd just start giving a lesson." Godin spent a few weeks on finance, and a few weeks on creativity and art. The lectures were "personal, direct and interactive. There was an opportunity to engage and ask questions." Students would write a daily blog entry about their experiences, and Godin would assign projects, and the students would come up with their own.

"Doing it," Godin called it. "Picking up the phone, making the plan, signing the deal," he wrote, describing the mojo of his altMBA program. "Pushing 'publish.' Announcing. Shipping...We spent a lot of time on this area. Every morning, each person came in prepared to push someone in the group to overcome the next hurdle. This is what growth looks like, and it was energizing to be a part of it."

Allan was impressed by these real-world experiments, the way Godin knocked people out of their comfort zones. One of his fellow classmates was a talented painter, but like many artists she was afraid to sell. Godin threw her to the lions with an assignment. The young woman had to go to Grand Central Station to sell bibles. She was anything but religious, but she went to the crazily busy station in the belly of New York, and sell she did.

Experts in health care, publishing, the web, networking, and entrepreneurship delivered guest lectures. Godin took the class on field trips, including "a detailed exploration of the fabled Stew Leonard's supermarket" and "an engagement with maestro Roger Nierenberg at the Essex." Godin was creating the opposite of what he'd experienced at Stanford earning his MBA in the 80s, where he "spent a lot of time reading irrelevant case studies and even more time building complex financial models," hours he felt were wasted for the modern entrepreneur. "The rest of the time, it's about shipping, motivating, leading, connecting, envisioning and engaging," Godin wrote on his blog, describing his program. "So that's what we worked on."

In an age flush with traditional MBA programs, professional accelerators and incubators, there was something remarkable about how overnight Godin created his very own entrepreneurial ecosystem, a tight group of very talented individuals who came together, quite literally in his space, for his improvised program, and left energized to make stuff happen. People like Clay Hebert, who became an expert in crowdfunding, and the fear-conquering Ishita Gupta, who founded the entrepreneurial fear.less magazine. Allan hoped to pick up some of Godin's product mastery. "I wanted to be a product guy, a builder. I wanted to be like Seth in terms of creating companies." Godin had sold a company for $30 million during the dotcom days to Yahoo, created a hot website, and published more than a dozen books, many of them bestsellers.

"I gained a lot," said Allan of the program that was so popular that it was extended to nine months. "Working with Seth was a life-changing experience." Allan learned about personal bravery, being willing to fail, and something totally new. The Marine Corps had taught him many things, but art was not one of them. "Seth taught me that art is not just painting or sculpture. Seth's definition was that art is anything that changes the way you think about the world."

The Marines had thrust Allan into a tight knit culture that was all about leadership. Now he was learning that leadership could come from ideas. "Seth talked about what you wanted to be. What impact you wanted to make in an ideal world, what would you do? I loved it. And if you thought you had an answer, he'd push you to make it bigger."

Allan had a knack for rejecting the obvious, for following his gut and heart, for finding the places and people that inspired him. He'd found a camaraderie in the Marine Corps and he was loving Seth Godin's altMBA, an ecosystem seemingly created out of thin air. Allan wanted more. It was time to come home to San Francisco.

The Conductor

Carlos Cooks Up a Surprise

If ever there was a metaphor for the tremendous pressure of a startup, the insane all-in, madcap lurch toward the launch, this was it, being rushed to San Francisco General with a full-blown panic attack. Carlos had every right to panic – the excruciating delays in opening, the massive bills for rent, complicated architecture, infrastructure, and improvements piling up, the scary family fights over what was shaping up to be a financial disaster. But fortunately, Carlos quickly recovered, and at long last the SoMa StrEat Food Park opened. And just like that, he instantly had something new to fret about.

The park was packed. Fantastic news that brought a new stress. Going into the business, Carlos was acutely aware that he was creating a food experience for which there was no blueprint. He had no advance proof that this was a concept that would work long-term. Now that it had caught fire with the public, he encountered something he'd never expected. Ambivalence and inconsistency on the supply side. Some days Carlos could only attract five or six trucks instead of a full ten-truck line-up. Some days the trucks couldn't handle the demand. Making every day a struggle to meet demand.

Carlos wanted trucks to commit to showing up every day, but many weren't prepared to be permanent residents. They didn't know if the park would survive. This made scheduling a challenge, but as the crowds grew over the long, unusually sunny summer, Carlos's success began attracting San Francisco's hottest trucks. Eventually he even figured out how to squeeze in eleven trucks. Since few would commit to the whole week, Carlos improvised, revamping his business model around variety and discovery. Offering some new trucks every day meant that he could stoke his growing social media following by teasing out news of the day's trucks – much like a restaurant's daily specials — and entice nearby tech workers to visit the park regularly.

The park demonstrated how entrepreneurism invites risk and serendipity. You might have imagined this was a fixed food truck park with a set way of doing business. But he was fashioning a new sort of Place that thrived through flexibility. It was his canvas, and just as Jackson Pollock let paint fly, Carlos experimented with his unusual place. He partnered with the events website Funcheap, brought in big-screen TVs for the San Francisco Giants' 2012 World Series, and two thousand fans showed up during each game to eat and drink from his bar. That Halloween, Carlos charged $5 a head, and four thousand revelers came and danced in the rain — with a line of another thousand revelers twisting around the block, hoping to get in. "That was absolute madness," said Carlos. "The cops told us it was so big that it was causing traffic jams in the city." Carlos began sensing that whatever this thing was, there was no doubt that it was becoming far more than just a place to eat, and by leapfrogging from the family tapas restaurants to this novel concept, Carlos was inventing an entirely new category.

Soon Airbnb, Zynga, One Kings Lane, Intel, and other companies were paying Carlos generous fees to rent out the park for evening parties. It's funny, but this former abandoned lot was not long ago home to addicts and rats, a swatch of concrete next to a freeway ramp, a forlorn place that shouted "nowhere." Now, under Carlos's vision, it was becoming a hot destination, a new kind of third place.

The Collaborator
Joe Revs his Engines in Motor City

Joe Boggio grew up in a one-stoplight town. He was sheltered and shy, but he busted out. Tracking upward to high school, university, leading a Toastmasters chapter, and earning a highly marketable degree in engineering. And now, after college, he was beginning to feel...he had it made! After his months-long experiment flipping the tables to interview dozens of recruiters and potential bosses to land the perfect job, he said "yes sir!" to IBM for a starting salary of $42,000 a year, making the move from his college town of East Lansing to the suburbs of Detroit. This was the late 90s, when "tech was becoming tech," and Joe was pinching himself about his good fortune. *Game over*, he thought to himself. *Life changer! I'm rich! This is crazy money.*

Pretty much every one of his fellow two dozen recruits in his onboarding program had the same reaction: their careers were set. Even better, IBM eased them into their sales jobs with a long and generous onboarding process. Presenters would offer overviews of computer servers, operating systems, or integrated software, prepping them for the day they'd head out into the field. But for now, for the next six months, there was no meeting with customers, no sales quota, no trial and error. No rejection. It was an insulated, supportive corporate culture, a perspective that acknowledged it takes some time to figure yourself out when you're 21.

Gradually, Joe and his fellow onboarders began working with mentors, shadowing them on sales calls, learning the ropes. The mentor's job was to suss out their interests and strengths to best place them within IBM's ranks. Joe got slotted into an SAP hardware specialist role, helping to match clients to the best computer servers to handle their enterprise software workloads.

IBM's big Midwest clients were automotive-related, and as

an engineer cutting his chops in sales, Joe quickly demonstrated a knack for translating technical terms into clear, intelligible English to auto executives. He began with a Collaborator's strategy: setting up meetings with executives to glean insights, immersing himself in the culture of the automotive industry. He sensed a seismic change afoot, that the edge for a car maker was becoming more about the electronics and software hidden inside. Joe knew things about emerging technologies that the automotive execs didn't know they needed to know. Being blindsided wasn't in anyone's best interests. Not for the companies. Not for Joe. So he started to help Chrysler innovate. It took them three years to get a car to market. Joe wanted to cut that down to one.

Joe found a kindred spirit in Chrysler's Chief Innovation Officer. They would meet and talk shop about the tech in the cars. Chrysler in its early days had been an innovator on the software used to design vehicles, but years of cost-cutting had turned the pivotal system into a shadow of its former technical self. Joe and other IBM software reps were trying to push product upgrades without a clear view of the overall system. Chrysler's silos didn't help. The procurement team's software didn't work with the accounting team's, or the product development's team, or the engineering team's. Joe saw, listened, and acted. The Collaborator in him built a community of the half dozen stakeholders essential to the next wave of the solution. It worked. And when he left IBM to go to Oracle a year later just as Y2K was coming down the pike, he brought Chrysler along with him.

The funny thing was that for a former extreme introvert, Joe was succeeding in large part through his ability to choreograph human networks that became his Place wherever he went. Joe relished making the connections that others couldn't. Inspiring people to collaborate and solve seemingly intractable issues. Corporate innovation was becoming his trademark.

Microsoft was next.

The Evangelist
Uwe Plumbs the Past for Inspiration

Years of making and marketing medical devices had turned Uwe into a subject matter expert. Microlife was manufacturing hundreds of thousands of thermometers and other medical devices for numerous brands throughout Europe, among them Spengler, a company with an intriguing legacy that caught Uwe's eye.

Many nations lay claim to inventing the blood pressure monitor, but according to Uwe, France awarded that honor to the Spengler company in 1907. Uwe's interest in Spengler went beyond the historical. He met the owners, and then designed and manufactured a range of digital blood pressure monitors for the company until he spied a buying opportunity, at which point he independently acquired the 100-year-old company. The Evangelist in Uwe saw that there could be many more products down the road, especially as he dove into rebranding Spengler to highlight the importance of corporate identity and legacy: "I worked a lot on the historical side, on France being the cradle of medical civilization. Pasteur, Marie Curie, the nephrology, tropical diseases, all that kind of stuff."

Uwe inherited the company's vast hoard of antique medical devices, which spurred him to become an avid collector, in part because it was a window into the creative process. "When you have that entire collection, you can see the evolution of technology," he said. "You can see why the blood pressure monitor was invented in three or four different countries at the same time. It was a logical next step. It's a beautiful tool for historical research."

Uwe set about to create a virtual Place of ideas and knowledge, one that would inspire him just as much as a city or a community. He collected and curated a treasure trove of far more than just blood pressure monitors. His cache eventually grew to a diverse mix of 3,500 medical devices, some iconic and transformative, some curiosities, all in one fashion or another providing a larger context. They broadened his sense of how ideas bubble up and get shared, affording him a chance to time-travel to gain a visceral and mental understanding of the many twists and turns along the path of innovation.

Highly focused interest magnifies knowledge and expertise. That was another advantage to being an Evangelist. Uwe was not a doctor or a clinician, but his experience was becoming an asset, one he smartly learned to parlay. He had become a recognized authority in the management of peripheral arterial disease simply because he had analyzed blood pressure for so long that he'd developed encyclopedic knowledge. Domain expertise by any other name. And his collection was foundational. Mastery of a single subject gave him the confidence to hunt the next big thing. "There's no such thing as an invention today. Everything is derived, everything is a natural evolution of what was there before," argued Uwe, who knew that his collection was far more than a hobby. It was his compass.

"There's nothing better to predict the future than to look at the past."

Takeaways:
Discovering your Place

Place. The right people, connections and environment to nourish your soul and dreams. Perhaps no stage is more individual. What Face guides you to your best Place?

Makers build Places.
Outsiders know two good Places can be better than one.
Accidentals happen into the right Place and stay.
Guardians connect Place with mission.
Visionaries follow their nose.
Athletes thrive in the wild.
Leaders study how communities are made.
Conductors learn how to draw crowds.
Collaborators take stock of key partners.
Evangelists turn ideas and artifacts into virtual Places.

The Launch

"Don't try, there is only doing.
Find what you need to be doing, by doing."
– Perry Klebahn

The Launch is about action. Creating targeted prototypes and experiments. Connecting with real, paying customers earlier than you thought possible. Often before you even have a product. Discovering that rapid-fire, iterative experiments build knowledge and light the path to success.

Let's review how far you've come. The Awakening is the first brush of enlightenment. The Shift, the crucial initial commitment. The Place, the inherent understanding that people, place, resources, and attitudes are essential to nourish this massive undertaking. And now here we are at The Launch, where the rubber truly hits the road.

We all are individuals, with our unique talents, strengths, and weaknesses, and so it's not surprising that we all call upon different means to summon the energy, enthusiasm, and commitment necessary to take charge. Some start by doing, diving in and taking action without pausing to question themselves. Others start by knowing, gradually gaining the confidence to find the right partners and opportunities as they embrace their chosen path. And, still others start by feeling. They follow their gut, and tap their emotions to make deep, often intuitive connections with followers drawn into their orbit as they pursue their dream.

The Launch is serious business. It requires daily commitment, the grown-up version of the *Little Engine That Could* mantra, "I think I can, I think I can." This is no longer simply about a Shift in mindset, an exploration, or a move to a fresh Place, a new and stimulating atmosphere and environment. What's different about this stage is the public accountability. People are watching. And there are often others on board who depend on us to keep going.

There will be scary, deer-in-the-headlights moments when we kick ourselves for leaving security behind. This is where bravery counts, where action replaces hesitation. The Launch demands too that we make peace with our vulnerability, the ever-present specter of failure. Countries, cities and cultures have widely different tolerances for failure, which is why as we've seen, your ecosystem and community are so essential. Our natural fear of making mistakes, of failing before our peers, mentors, family and society at large, can hold us back from trying. Which is not to say these fears ever totally fall away. We just find a way to counter that fear with courage.

It's easy to recognize someone who's starting by doing. They're moving fast. They prototype more than they plan. Doers quickly learn how to break complex tasks down into small, individual elements. They learn by testing what works and what doesn't. They dive into the why, quickly discerning what they might change.

This flexibility of mind, this openness to shifting course, is no small challenge. Launching requires confidence and trust. The strength to stand up to naysayers. The resilience to overcome the obstacles that lie ahead.

Launching by Doing can be bracing at first, a bit like jumping into a frigid, raging river. But that's why we're lucky.

Doers teach us a lot about doing.

The Maker

Perry Targets the Customer

How did Perry Klebahn and Michael Dearing start Launchpad? They took the time to understand their customers' true wants and needs. First, they smartly made their class a non-required course, avoiding coasting juniors or seniors filling a prerequisite on autopilot. They had a course number and a name: ME301 Launchpad. But how to find the right students, the right teams? "It started with the idea that we needed to recruit, that we needed to get the word out, and we needed a place to meet people," recalled Perry. "One thing that was very humbling was that we had to clarify what the class was all about."

Professors don't generally pitch students, but Perry and Michael did a road show. They hit up the most promising groups – the Engineering Club, the Computer Science Club, the Business Association of Stanford Entrepreneurial Students (BASES) and Stanford's Graduate School of Business. They pitched an intensive 10-week action-oriented, customer- and sales-centric accelerator. Launchpad was designed for student teams hungry to incorporate, to quickly notch sales and traction, and then come June, bust out of Stanford.

How did this prototype go? Out of the nine teams in the inaugural cohort of April of 2010, three failed, three became moderately successful, and three were home runs. There was Ben Knelman, a Russian studies major, who recruited and then texted with a dozen Stanford janitors to help them learn how to save money. Knelman tapped behavioral economics, psychology and advanced gamification to turn Juntos into a global market leader for millions of underserved international financial services customers. Main Street Hub, started by two Stanford MBA's, also began with empathy for an ignored customer, targeting small businesses that struggle with social media.

GoDaddy ultimately purchased the startup for $175 million in cash and future payouts.

Akshay Kothari and Ankit Gupta perhaps best exemplified how Launchpad accelerated the Launch. On April 3, 2010, the very first week of Launchpad, Steve Jobs introduced the iPad. The two bright Stanford computer science graduate students had a prescient idea for a mobile news aggregation app for the device. Hewing to Launchpad's mantra – iterate fast and get it in front of customers – Kothari and Gupta first prototyped their Pulse app on paper sketches, then Keynote slides. Their laboratory was a Palo Alto coffee shop, ideal to directly gain in-person feedback on their remarkably well-designed visual interface. In May, before Launchpad's 10 weeks ended, Pulse was in the App Store, and a few weeks later Steve Jobs promoted it onstage at Apple's Worldwide Developers Conference. Pulse quickly became the App Store's number-one bestseller. Three years later the 20-something engineers would sell their upstart to LinkedIn for $90 million in cash and stock. All told, unparalleled success from a single cohort from a brand-new college accelerator with a part-time staff of two adjunct professors: three companies that would soon be valued at more than a quarter-billion dollars. And that, somewhat incredibly, was just Launchpad's first year.

The Outsider

Daniel Enters the Chocolate Factory

Daniel and Nik did it – they made it into Launchpad!

Daniel was in heaven relishing the break from the monochromatic law school grind. "The d.school is a different physical space. It doesn't feel like anything else on campus. I felt like I'd entered Willy Wonka's Chocolate Factory."

Daniel was also making a distinct statement about the seriousness of his intentions, not what you'd expect from the son of two lawyers who would soon be cramming for the bar exam. "Law school and medical schools are not like the other schools at Stanford. You don't have free time," Perry explained, looking back on this time. "So for Daniel and Nik to enter Launchpad, to commit to it even for a couple of weeks, they'd crossed a hurdle that many of the other entrepreneurs hadn't." The Chocolate Factory vibe wasn't just about being immersed in Stanford's hip d.school, surrounded by animated students working on a rainbow of design-centric projects illustrated by poster boards festooned with post-its, photos of users, and experiential drawings. Launchpad plunged them into an intensely focused accelerator with eight other dynamic teams. Daniel saw one fact clearly: half the class had working prototypes. A few had customers.

On day one of Stanford Launchpad that April of 2012, Daniel, Nik, and the other student founders were asked to put on the hat of a venture capitalist. Everyone was given a pot of imaginary cash to invest in the other teams. Incredibly, Daniel and Nik were ecstatic to discover that they were at the top of the list. But there was something Perry and Michael didn't say. Winning this popularity contest was often fool's gold. Often those ranked near the bottom of the list worked harder and ended up on top. The class was about doing. While Daniel and Nik's paper prototype got them into the class, and their classmates saw tremendous potential in their idea, the two law students were quickly hit with a sobering challenge. Now they had to deliver a functioning prototype. In just two weeks.

Back in the fall, Daniel had realized that a business plan was not a product, and had begun to wade into another part of the Stanford ecosystem, competing for the attention of computer science students, the big fish on a campus where tech expertise was gold. It was discouraging. Neither Daniel nor his co-founder, Nik, had the right connections. "People are working on other projects, and you've got to convince them to join yours. We didn't have a good personal network of people who had the right skills," he said. "So, it was all meeting strangers, or friends of friends, which takes time."

Daniel had hacked out a classic Outsider's method: He crashed the advanced masters-level data visualization course demo days. They were high-tech show-and-tells. Students would showcase their work on poster boards, and Daniel would "wander through, and see the different projects, and follow up with an email to folks who seemed like they were touching on something related, either working with textual documents, or network visualizations." Facing the Launchpad deadline, Daniel and Nik circled back to the three or four engineers with whom they'd had more serious conversations the past few months. "Hey, let's put together a weekend hackathon," they proposed. "We'll buy food and coffee and Red Bull, and let's build a prototype!" No money at all, no offer of anything more than spending your Stanford weekend hacking out code.

Four engineers said yes. An intrigued undergrad, two master's students, and a PhD candidate excited about their problem.

Daniel's business plan was about to get real, which was a good thing because the rest of the class seemed well on their way. Two computer science dudes were off and running with CodeHS, a novel web-based way to teach coding at high schools, and a young woman was already selling children's bible stories for the iPad. To Daniel some of the ideas were wild. Take LifeSwap, a concept Perry thought hilarious. "They were a really funny team with the idea that you'd basically swap jobs with somebody." Crazy as it sounded, LifeSwap was quickly up and running. "They had sign-ups," said Perry. "In the Valley, people really want to do this stuff." And then there was Man Crates, led by Jon Beekman, a big, charismatic former Stanford MBA and Fulbright scholar. Beekman was curating manly stuff like beef jerky in an ammo can, hunting gear, or tool sets. He'd stick the loot in a "Man Crate" with a crow bar. Gifting for men barely existed, and Beekman hoped to deliver a masculine, playful new gift box experience that would scale.

Launchpad taught students to activate new entrepreneurial muscles, to skip jogging and dash right into sprints, to cram into 10 weeks the bursts of energy, focus, experiments and actions needed to gain critical orbital momentum. The Man Crates team helped teach the whole cohort how to get started. "Demand harvesting," Perry dubbed it. Beekman was running a flurry of Google and Facebook ads, experiments to see what macho product mixes and marketing resonated. "They would put up a fake product page for the crate," explained Perry. "You could buy the zombie apocalypse crate, you could buy the beer one. They were really smart to do it, and it made a huge impact on the class." Nothing was real, except the direct connection with customers, the testing of people's willingness to buy. "They could put up creative [ads] for all these crates at different prices," said Perry. "They almost had this NASA-like data set really quickly, and they hadn't actually built anything."

Daniel and Nik found it both exhilarating and more than a little bit intimidating to be in class with the likes of Man Crates and the computer science majors launching CodeHS. So many teams not only had a clear brand and a robust prototype, but the robust entrepreneurial skills that they so patently lacked. Yet part of the magic of Launchpad was the momentum gained by the collective journey. That abundant energy and enthusiasm opened their eyes to the possible.

That weekend in mid-April, Daniel and Nik brought their volunteer programmers an ample supply of pizza, coffee, and Red Bull to

Stanford's spacious d.school studios for their makeshift hackathon. Taking Michael's instruction to heart, they'd managed to get their hands on a digital copy of 50,000 Supreme Court cases. Their programmers hacked out a simple search mechanism with a primitive UX. You could type in a query, say "enemy combatants," and see a visual representation of the network of cases. "It was really ugly," said Daniel. "It looked like a giant plate of spaghetti."

Two weeks before, their Launchpad classmates had picked their legal research startup as the most likely to succeed. Now the class repeated the voting ritual, and the other team's prototypes were clearly far more sophisticated. "People saw our prototype, and they're like, 'I don't get this,'" said Daniel. "'If this is your idea, it stinks.'"

The law students finished dead last. But oddly enough Daniel and Nik were not the least bit discouraged. Under Perry and Michael's guidance, they'd made rapid progress, building a functioning piece of technology in just two weeks. And something else was happening. Each new experience and skill was bleeding into another. Daniel and Nik were on multiple, intertwined paths. Launchpad was simultaneously helping them advance through the university's business plan competition. Breezing through the early rounds, they'd improved their pitch, and now boasted something few other contestants could match, a working tech prototype for what they believed was a very big idea. They might be at the bottom of the heap in Launchpad, but they were gaining confidence in Stanford's 150-team business plan competition.

They just might make the finals.

The Evangelist
Uwe Prototypes the Peltier Effect

Uwe was ready to try something new, which in many ways was his normal way of being, as he was pretty much always trying something new. Popular mythology often paints entrepreneurs as inspired by a fresh insight, laser-focused on the target customer and shaped by market forces. But Uwe was cut from an earlier generation, a salty blend of marketer, hustler, entrepreneur and inventor. Uwe had made, designed, improved or marketed so many devices in his day that dreaming up new ones and tinkering with prototypes was as natural as breathing.

Speed and fluency for Uwe came not from some lean, mean approach, but rather from a lyrical style – simply riffing, and quickly making stuff – without fretting whether any particular experiment might morph into an actual product. Uwe was an idea man, one whose ideas often first bobbed up as physical objects.

Most of these prototypes went into Uwe's "drawer," a real place in his workshop but also a metaphor for the subconscious of a feverish, yet happy creator. At any one time ten to fifteen models filled Uwe's drawer. Many had market potential, some were inspired by whimsy, and others were missing an essential element. Play and work intermingled. Uwe had patience and an acute understanding of larger currents. Often it wasn't the right time for Uwe, or for the device, but that didn't stop his creative impulse. Inspiration could strike anytime, such as during a fateful trip with his brother to Provence in 2003. One night, his brother handed his insulin to a staff member at their hotel, requesting that it be refrigerated. The next day, they discovered it had been stuck in the freezer. There was moment of panic and scrambling, until fortunately they lucked into a finding an open pharmacy in time. But the near-catastrophe got Uwe thinking.

A few days later, at Uwe's flat in Paris, the brothers dove into that pain point, and over a bottle of Bordeaux sketched out a concept with the potential to help millions. A tiny, portable fridge, not just to carry insulin but any of the hundreds of other new, modern medicines that require refrigeration. The design rested, not surprisingly, in a principle Uwe knew from his expansive study of inventions, the Peltier Effect. Explained Uwe: "If you take cubes of metal of different density and pass current through them, the friction will cause super heat on one side and cooling on the other." Or, so went the theory. Uwe cobbled together a crude working prototype, powered by a battery he pulled out of a Sony video cam. "It was something we tossed off," he said. "For private use."

Uwe, as usual, was juggling multiple ventures. Busy with his medical devices company, Microlife, and launching a new med-tech enterprise, iHealth, he thought of the brick-sized fridge as little more than a potential insurance policy for his brother. But, as he often did with his latest creation, Uwe entered a competition. With over 4,000 applicants each year, NASA's prestigious Create the Future Design Contest wasn't just any old science competition. Nor was Uwe just any contestant. He took second prize. The FDA heralded the brothers' new life-saving invention on the front page of their digital newsletter. CNBC did a story, then primetime TV. "Suddenly we started getting hundreds and hundreds of emails from people who wanted to buy this product," said Uwe. "But the problem was that the product didn't exist. It was just a prototype."

The mini-fridge went into Uwe's drawer. Its time had yet to come.

The Athlete
Joel Puts His Theory in Motion

Joel had a powerful network. Money in the bank. Confidence that came from having a successful startup exit already under his belt. The history and experience to know that he could tackle any aspect of running a new business. The Athlete had time, ambition, resources, and most of all, the confidence he could pull this off. He could hire people for drawings and consultations. He didn't need outside investors. And he wasn't afraid to dive deeply into his idea. The garage was his first laboratory and his prototypes were primitive, just raw plywood, early attempts to go beyond the concept. Joel soon discovered his grandfather's beautiful tools weren't up to the task. Kurtis, the first designer he hired, did early sketches. Next came a cabinetry guy with a lathe to produce what they called the "pucks." They began to play with a curve that would stay within the "optimal radius to create enough movement to matter but not enough to distract." You had to be able to balance and still type easily.

Joel knew expert validation would bring his physics to the next level. At Teva, he'd worked regularly with Heeluxe. Dr. Geoffrey Gray, the founder and president, was a physical therapist with a background in woodworking and classic car mechanics who had created an elite laboratory that specialized in testing athletic shoes for major brands. Joel brought over his early prototypes to the lab near UC Santa Barbara, and Gray pulled together a reasonable sample size of testers. In a controlled experiment, subjects worked seated, on treadmills, and balancing on Joel's board.

They tested Joel's theory, that by introducing subtle rocking movements, the board would bring fun and motion into workers' office lives, and burn calories to boot. That shift would have to be measured. Too much motion and your typing might be impaired and your productivity decline. Gray came back with good news. Joel's theory was sound. The lateral movement burned significant calories without greatly diminishing keystroke productivity. The bad news: he was over-stretching the calf and the Achilles. So, the functional motion goal became, "How do you limit the dorsal and plantar flexion?" said Joel. "Your heel to toe. How can we stop you at about 16 degrees flexion?"

Joel also began focusing on keystroke productivity as a baseline test to balance raising your heart rate while maintaining productivity. Through dozens of iterations and testing, he found the "sweet spot," a 15% increase in energy expenditure, with a less than 1% decrease in keystroke productivity. The prototypes became easier to balance on, the over-flexion resolved. But now Joel feared his board was starting to look clunky. And that's where the timely introduction from his former creative director came into play. Utility wasn't sufficient. The board had to inspire, like the sloping lines of a sports car, the elegant minimalism of the iPhone, or as Joel dreamed, like a classic New York skyscraper. "We really wanted to look at the emotional aspects. How would it be art, not equipment, and that's where we worked with Jonas, and he turned me on to an industrial designer who was in between gigs and we just had a lot of fun. The challenge was how do you make this beautiful? How do you make it iconic, something that's as worthwhile standing up as it is sitting on the floor?"

Joel met Dave Malina, the recently transplanted New York designer, and they clicked, "had a good kinship" and just "started throwing ideas together." Joel already knew all the angles and geometry he wanted, how much tipping would be desirable. What was going on "underfoot" was very clear. The task for Malina was, "'Help me make this look beautiful. Because it just feels like something you'd get at a hardware store right now.' And he came back with three visual concepts but also different manufacturing processes as well. That's where it all started to come together. Very quickly. It went from, 'Oh this is interesting,' to 'Holy crap, we have something!'"

The Accidental

Mait Juggles Techstars

If Mait had known what he was getting himself into he might have thought twice about cutting short his rising career as an elite physicist at CERN. But in the fall of 2013, he bid adieu to the world-famous laboratory and moved back to Estonia. Launching a startup, he was fast discovering, was a full-time job – and then some. He'd naively imagined they could sneak by with a single developer. Then quickly realized they needed businesspeople, more developers, linguists, designers, not to mention loads of cash, management expertise and time. Juggling balls is how some describe the early stages of a startup. Mait was finding it hard not to drop some.

Yet there were bright opportunities on the horizon, starting with the far-fetched dream of winning a coveted spot at Techstars in London. Fifteen hundred teams had applied for a dozen precious spots in the renowned accelerator, and Lingvist had also been invited to pitch in early December at Slush, the Nordics' hottest tech conference, just across the Baltic Sea.

Choosing the right, early investors is one of the best ways for a startup to gain traction, and Jaan Tallinn proved that truism in the quiet, magnetic way he pulled human and financial capital into their orbit, starting with Tanel Hiir, a gifted developer and core technical team leader at Skype. Tanel was looking for a fresh challenge, and that fall he invested in Lingvist and became its Chief Technology Officer, in one stroke guaranteeing Lingvist a talent pipeline. Tanel's Skype colleagues began making inquiries, and suddenly Mait had his pick of elite programmers eager to join. Things were happening fast, sometimes all at once.

The intensive Techstars interview process was in full swing right while Mait was hustling to raise his first angel round. He aimed for €200K, then quickly realized €300K wasn't outside the realm of possibility, then €400K, then €450K, and just like that, they'd closed a €600K round, triple what he'd planned. The interviews with Techstars were progressing well, thanks in part to having brought onboard a CTO with Tanel's impressive pedigree. Then, Mait suddenly discovered that one of the balls had inadvertently dropped. Just after the last Techstars interview, they realized that some of their investor commitments were conditional. One key VC had a conflict, and could not invest, and so several other investors pulled out, and Lingvist's funding package unraveled, dropping precipitously from €600K right back down to €200K.

Mait panicked. He was a physicist. He had no financial or business background. He was a rookie when it came to fundraising, and as for Techstars, more than ninety-nine percent of applicants were rejected. Maybe quitting CERN had been rash. There were some anxious days and sleepless nights, and then Jaan Tallinn demonstrated the extraordinary reach of his network. He typed out a few sentences, sharing the idea of Lingvist within a very small and exclusive chat group of key Skype founders and developers. Poof, like magic, "I had six meetings in one day," said Mait, "and all of them, during the meeting, said they wanted to invest."

Mait and Ott headed over on the ferry from Tallinn to nearby Helsinki for Slush, fatefully, just when Hiroshi Mikitani, the CEO of Rakuten, a Japanese e-commerce and Internet giant, asked to stop by Lingvist's Tallinn office. Mikitani had a unique, personal interest in accelerated language learning. Unbeknownst to Lingvist, he had recently mandated that all of his nearly 10,000 employees had to master English. He too was in Helsinki for Slush, and the President of Estonia had invited him to tour a few select startups in nearby Tallinn. Mait and Ott asked Tanel to cover for them, a classic case of a scrappy startup team "juggling the balls", except that Tanel was the archetypal introvert programmer. He refused to be publicly photographed and fiercely guarded his anonymity. Handling a high stakes pitch meeting with a potential ideal customer and investor all by his lonesome? Not so fast. Tanel pushed back that he didn't even own a proper suit. Reluctantly, with some encouragement from Ott and Mait, Tanel pulled his high school graduation suit out of storage, a bit tight and short, since he'd gained some pounds and height. Tanel met the Japanese executive and read him the Lingvist pitch off the screen in his thick Estonian accent, and everyone quickly forgot all about Rakuten.

Over at Slush, Mait, with virtually no experience as a public speaker, took to the stage in the artificial haze and exaggerated near-darkness at the cult-like conference. His pitch – promoting an AI-inspired breakthrough in accelerated language learning – was a hit, and instantly they were flush with potential investors. Then came more good news: They'd been accepted into Techstars. They scouted out a London Airbnb crashpad for Mait and a few team members for the next three months of intense mentoring, MBA must-know business basics, and the fine art of pitching investors. On the flight over from Tallinn, Mait made a brief stop in Helsinki and met with a Finnish investor, and promptly picked up another €200K commitment. Lingvist had over a million euros in the bank, a sum that struck Mait as enormous. It seemed they could do no wrong. Mait wondered why they were even bothering with Techstars, an accelerator highly focused on attracting funding for its carefully culled startups.

The Accidental would soon find out why.

The Collaborator
Joe Engineers His Dream Job

First IBM, then Oracle, now Microsoft.

Joe's curiosity, hunger to learn, and people skills were earning him exciting new positions, and a hint of the new powerful software in development that could give companies a tremendous competitive edge. But that wasn't technically his job as head of global sales for DaimlerChrysler, one of Microsoft's biggest accounts. Joe was trying to sell things that were not for sale, overstepping his job description, right into making himself an attractive candidate for a new position – outside of Microsoft.

Was this Joe's big break? The closest he had to an advisor was his boss. His old boss was trying to recruit him for yet another company. Joe laid it on the table: "I just got this great offer. I don't know what to do." Joe was lucky. His boss took it in stride. "Go home. Think about it. Have a glass of wine. Come back tomorrow morning and let's talk about what you'd do if you had your dream job. If you want to pursue a job elsewhere, OK. But if you want to stay and do something different here I'll help you with that."

Joe didn't sleep much that night. What if Microsoft would give him the freedom to create a brand-new innovation division? He came back in the morning with a bold roadmap. How he – former introvert and current tech sales guy Joe Boggio – would build an innovation SWAT team within Microsoft. He slid it across the table. His boss didn't even glance at the plan. "Done. Start next week."

Joe pushed back, "Don't you want to read this?"

"I don't need to. I know this is what you want to do. Oh, and another thing, I want you to speak at this conference." Joe couldn't believe it. He'd gotten his dream job, the chance to take his vision center stage. But as the day of the conference drew nearer, he panicked. The audience would top a thousand. Bill Gates was recording a video to kick it off, and Joe would follow the US Secretary of Energy.

Joe walked back into his boss's office. Maybe he wasn't the right guy. His boss got up, closed the door, and got in his face "'I just put my career on the line for you to put you in this role and you're chickening out? Get a spine. You're gonna do this!" Then, Joe showed him the agenda. 'Oh yeah,' he huffed. "You're way outgunned here. 'Sit down, we're gonna spend a few hours anchoring some messages."'

Joe barely slept the two days before the event. At the end of his 30-minute panel discussion, the execs from IBM and Motorola leaned over: "Can I get a copy of your card? I want to talk more about what you're doing." Just like that, Joe had just successfully pitched his massive intrapreneurial venture to the titans of the industry.

All he had to do was make it happen. Which turned out to be a different thing altogether: "We went through this whole exercise to build a concept, a prototype, and then at the end we brought it to a client, and it was a very notable, global client. They looked at the product and were like, 'We've had that kind of technology for four years.' So we spent all this energy and had all these double PhDs coming up with a concept, and they were like, 'Where have you been? You didn't look around you first? You didn't come talk to us first? We know that market. We know that technology. We know that customer. We've put our own billions into market research around that. We forgot more than you think you know about our market."'

It was a humbling experience, but Joe could be forgiven for making a few rookie mistakes. This was just 2007. Eric Ries's revolutionary *The Lean Startup* hadn't yet been published. The field of innovation strategy was expanding rapidly, and Joe went back to the drawing board, hungry and curious, devouring everything he could get his hands on. Many of the most prominent authors and speakers taught at executive programs at Berkeley, MIT, Wharton, and Harvard. Joe spliced together his own custom applied master's degree, seeking out these gurus, attending a different program each year, gleaning precisely what he needed to learn in bite-sized pieces.

Joe couldn't possibly do this alone. The Collaborator found the ideal partner in Microsoft Research's teams and labs. Together, they had an ambitious goal: to create a collaborative, invitation-only group to tackle big trends just in their infancy – cloud, social, mobile, privacy. They wanted to bring together leaders from iconic companies with a commitment to research and scientific advancement. They called it the Microsoft Innovation Outreach Program. They aimed high, straight for the top decision makers, hoping to skip past geeky IT gurus and draw both chief technology officers and marketing chiefs from Fortune 500 companies.

This wasn't about imposing Microsoft's will but rather creating a place and experience to share insights. The peer-to-peer, co-creation approach attracted 16 attending corporations for the initial two-day experience in Redmond in the Spring of 2009. The first year wasn't perfect. While they got a top executive from the prestigious 3M, many of the other company's delegations weren't at the same stature. But by the following year they were starting to attract the top executives, and then it took off and became a full-fledged program with multiple events a year, participants divided into parallel cohorts to reduce competitive concerns. The Innovation Outreach Program quickly grew to 35 participating companies – major banks, manufacturers, retailers, oil and gas – representing over $2 trillion in annual revenue. Joe had his hands full. He rose to Director of Innovation for the US Commercial Sector at Microsoft. More and more of Microsoft's clients were coming to the company's extensive briefing center, and Joe helped formalize and create the company's point of view on innovation. But as far as he'd come, he saw limitations. Microsoft innovation revolved, naturally, around Microsoft solutions.

The pattern was repeating. Joe began to wonder if he needed a new Place.

The Visionary
Risto Plants His Flag

P alo Alto was about to become Risto's Place, his wild dream to move Ideam to California finally coming true. This was pretty much a miracle. "It's important to remember that the only way to get out of Finland was to be an employee of Nokia or some other big company. Small companies like mine couldn't afford to send people abroad." But that summer night in 2012, the company celebrated at an offsite, a raucous night of cheering, drinking and fun. In the morning, a groggy Risto arrived at the embassy in Helsinki to pick up his visa and three others for the initial team moving to California. He'd paid a Big Four consulting firm to manage the process. He'd been assured everything would go smoothly. They were wrong: the visas had been rejected. Risto couldn't believe it, and the minute he left the embassy he blew up and screamed at the consultants. This was really, really bad news. "When you get declined," he said, "it's in your records forever."

The timing was terrible. Risto had several cool clients waiting in California, multiple $100,000-plus projects lined up that they now lost because they were stuck in Finland. Risto fired the consulting firm and hired a Finnish woman to try again. A month passed, two, then three. Five months later the Finnish woman achieved what the US consulting firm couldn't. They got their visas, arrived in December, and got to work.

Risto had a highly focused plan that was all about finding the perfect customers. Though he'd flown halfway across the globe, he wanted to plant seeds in a very small region emanating from his new, magic Palo Alto place. "I was looking at all the big clients, like Facebook, Google. All of them were here. I had this rule, I need to be able to ride my bike to reach my client. That was my focus, riding my bike. I'm not going to Seattle, or Los Angeles. Being in the Bay Area, and San Francisco, and everything between, that was my focus."

The strategy worked. Risto quickly began picking up meetings, and landed more deals, proving to himself and his team that the Palo Alto move was transformative. His finance guy had given him a goal of logging $1.1 million additional revenue during the first full year in California. Three months later, Risto took the local team out for a celebratory dinner on University Ave. He had exciting news. He'd beaten the yearly goal they'd given him in just three months. Risto was on a roll. Quickly notching over $1 million in sales might seem a modest success for many entrepreneurs, but it validated moving his small team all the way from Helsinki.

Those seeds he'd planted during earlier trips were starting to bear fruit. That small two-day workshop he'd done for the startup Sentilla had led to a substantial $100K job. But that was just the start. That $8,000 workshop turned out to have a lifetime value of over five million. "They were referring us to everyone they knew, without asking," said Risto. "Three board members called me. They were like, 'This is better than the iPhone.' And then I got everyone to refer us to their portfolio companies. And it just built from there."

The Conductor

Carlos Entertains an Exit

Carlos was tempted, tired, exhilarated, and more than a little bit confused. Just weeks after opening SoMa StrEat Food Park he'd received a takeover email inquiry from a major LA restaurant group. Food trucks were hot down south but the investors had yet to come up with a viable, money-making model, and they liked what this kid in San Francisco was doing. The executives flew up for a meeting. "It was intimidating and very scary," said Carlos. "All very suits, ties, financials, numbers." They got down to business. They'd buy him out for a million dollars and keep him on as a partner for $150K a year, huge money for the son of a restaurateur barely out of college. Exiting early would remove all the risk from running operations at the park. Carlos was unsure. Was this really why he'd taken this huge risk?

He kept negotiations open. The LA group did their due diligence, sending up a humorless man with one task: To count people coming and going to the park. He sat there for a whole month, and four months later, Carlos recalls, the executives flew back up and showed they had "more information about my park than I had. They knew my numbers better than I did." And that was scary too.

Carlos was deeply proud of what he'd created. Proud of how he'd overcome all the bureaucrats at City Hall to create something brand new in San Francisco, a new kind of place that was changing lives. Carlos was high on the momentum, on the gratitude of the small mom-and-pop truck-owners who saw him as this young new godfather of the emerging food truck biz. This entrepreneurial journey — it was bracing and hard and oh so risky, and the 24-year-old wanted more of it.

Carlos said no. The LA restaurant guys saw the numbers, the obvious business opportunities. Carlos had bigger ideas, ideas that he wanted to be the first to develop and scale.

Carlos was learning that variety and reach generates market power and the place he'd created, this new hub for food, had surprisingly broad potential. The Conductor's "let's give it a try" experimental approach – from throwing themed food festivals, to sports fan nights, dance classes, a mega Halloween party – was bringing thousands into the park, and that was huge. But he was also leading this expanding community, creating a more subtle network effect. Carlos, San Francisco's trusted pied piper of this new foodie revolution, was experimenting with a concept with even bigger potential, a new, pivotal role as a food truck broker. He already had relationships with 50 trucks, a number that was growing weekly. The orchestra was expanding, and the Bay Area was becoming his park. Tech firms, churches, hospitals, all manner of businesses and entities were coming to him. When he sent the trucks out to them, he took a cut, a booking fee.

Then, out of the blue, a tantalizing email popped into his inbox. Carlos had sworn he'd never open a second park. But the timing was good. SoMa was running smoothly. What harm was there in taking a meeting?

The Guardian
Karoli Names Her Baby

Singularity University had been a transformative experience for Karoli. She'd made great friends and contacts in California, and found inspiration for the next phase in her life. But she would not follow the typical track of a Silicon Valley entrepreneur. Karoli was expecting her first child, and when she returned home to Estonia, she took a year just for her daughter and herself. Time to enjoy motherhood, family and her long runs. Time when she tried to forget that flash of insight on her morning workout by the Google campus. The idea that her classmates had rejected: making it easier for people to work in the place of their dreams. Making it possible for other cities and countries to rival the Valley in attracting top tech talent.

Karoli's year dedicated to her daughter came and went, and she emerged with the conviction that "there are better ideas." She rode the ferry to Helsinki that November for Slush, which that year attracted 7,000 attendees, more than a hundred VCs and a thousand startups. Karoli handed out a whole package of business cards, and contemplated joining two different companies, one more established, the other so early that she might have been a co-founder. She toyed with a few other ideas. "The world had gotten so much freer about sex…there were so many gadgets," she noted, wondering why "Kickstarter doesn't even allow anything like that." She even went so far as to pitch the concept to a well-known venture capitalist she'd met through Singularity about creating an entire platform just for sex-related products. "No," was his blunt reaction. "That's not a very good idea."

In March of 2014, Karoli returned to the vision her Singularity teammates had summarily rejected. She hired a full-time nanny and bootstrapped from home, diving into research on her computer, and calls and emails to people in her network, experts in recruiting, startups in Silicon Valley. When she found a relevant article, Karoli would track down and quiz the writer or sources, putting to use her media savvy, her skill at finding experts. She set deadlines: find her co-founder by the end of April, have her pitch deck ready before June. She hired her technical co-founder fast, in mid-April, and he began coding that May. Karoli was bankrolling everything – including his salary – and the thousands she needed to invest would soon turn into tens of thousands.

The international job platform she envisioned would take plenty of tech to build, and she'd need capital fast. She'd been searching for weeks for the right name, thinking about how the startup she hoped to create was going "to merge our job and our dreams." One night it came to her. Why not connect the words "Job" and "Sabbatical?" She searched, and low and behold, the domain for Jobbatical was available, and even better, "nobody had mentioned the idea on the Internet." Sitting at her kitchen table, alone at 2 a.m., her husband and baby sound asleep, she smiled to herself at what seemed her good fortune: "I was double-happy."

Karoli had a great concept that could scale, the perfect name, a talented technical co-founder. She had found the mission and purpose so critical to a Guardian. She anticipated success and almost always the universe agreed, and her confidence had been proven right. By June, she'd scheduled her first investor pitch with EstBAN, the Estonian Business Angels Network. This part would be easy. She was a known entity in Estonia, respected for her teenage entrepreneurial success and impressive TV career.

What could go wrong?

The Leader
Allan Creates His Tribe

Fresh from Seth Godin's altMBA, Allan Young was ready to put his learnings into practice. Alex Krupp, his friend and fellow classmate, had just been accepted into the exclusive Y Combinator, and Allan climbed aboard for the ride. This was 2010, before the accelerator became legendary for its uncanny knack for selecting, mentoring, funding, and scaling hot startups. Still, it was red hot. Reddit was in Y Combinator's inaugural year, DropBox in its second, and just before Allan and Alex joined the accelerator in 2010, Stripe and Airbnb. Krupp and Allan had a big goal with LaunchHear, to develop software to help thousands of independent bloggers review products and make PR scale much like Google did with advertising.

Allan understood the power of culture. He'd joined the Marines, engaged with a neighboring university's business club with great success, thrived in Seth's altMBA, and now he was thrilled to enter Y Combinator. He had two objectives. Beyond launching another startup, he was curious about this radical model. Teams accepted into the program were staked $25,000, support and mentorship, with the wild hope that three months later they'd pitch on "demo day" and garner serious funding. "I wanted to see, 'How does this work?'" said Allan. "And I wanted to see how some brilliant young guy could create a product on the initial Y Combinator contribution of $25,000." Allan and Alex dove in, meeting with mentors, advisors, VCs, and fellow founders. Allan loved being part of a cohort, gaining energy and knowledge from the other startups, the excitement of seeing so many teams rushing to make stuff happen, and in that fertile hatchery of entrepreneurial mojo came a flash of inspiration, his next big idea.

First, a failure. LaunchHear, like most of that year's Y Combinator class, didn't gain traction. Then Allan and a friend teamed up with a private equity firm to put in a bid to buy MySpace, an effort he would later be happy failed. Allan and other investors would purchase and quickly sell the former home of Oakland's largest newspaper, the Tribune Tower.

But most of all, Allan would come to realize that it had been an honor and privilege to be backed by Y Combinator, an experience unlike any he'd had before in his first startup and the companies he'd scouted for investments. "Seeing all these startups come together on Tuesdays, you know, everybody's frantically building a product, getting ready for demo day," he recalled. "It was just a different process of building companies that I was accustomed to." Yet the philosopher in Allan knew that something had been sorely missing. He'd felt a pain. The full cohort would only convene at the accelerator's Mountain View office one evening a week. Allan craved more connection with his fellow batch mates. The other squads had so many talented technologists and entrepreneurs. That weekly meeting where they'd check in on all the teams, at once inspiring and motivating, left him hungry for more. Now that the experience had ended, he had an idea that captured his imagination.

The Leader in Allan set out to create his tribe, his own community, concepts instilled in him at Godin's altMBA. There was a beautiful irony at play in his whimsical, lyrical idea, less about money and more about planting seeds. This near-dropout, who'd refused to be hemmed in by the confines of his high school, was creating his own school for startups just a short walk from where his truancy and curiosity had drawn him into a hotel ballroom to find inspiration. As a skilled investor, attuned to trends and timing, Allan's gut told him it was time to invest in knowledge. Knowledge for others, knowledge for himself. He also quite simply was practicing what was becoming a personal mantra: *Never do the same thing twice in a row. Always be doing something new so that you can grow.*

Takeaways:
Launching

Rubber, meet road. It's time to go to market with your software or app. Ship product and go live. Launching requires that all-hands-on-deck mindset, when you absolutely need the right people. What Faces do you want on your team when you launch?

Makers find what they need to be doing by doing.
Outsiders attract talent from anywhere.
Evangelists work every possible publicity angle.
Collaborators start by listening.
Accidentals have an edge — the launch is unplanned.
Athletes trust in expert coaches.
Guardians lock in on their mission.
Conductors ramp up their platforms.
Visionaries set extreme goals to get traction.
Leaders build a tribe.

7

6

5 ——

The Money

Karoli had spent all her money. Her two co-founders had left their day jobs to follow her vision. She fretted. Had she led them astray? When the angels made their financial commitments she had imagined the process would be quick. "But then it turned out to be a contractual disaster." So nervous that she couldn't sleep, running out of savings, unsure whether she should or could get a business loan to get by, she found herself thinking, "What the hell am I doing here?"

4

3

2

1

Money, money, money. It feeds our families, powers economies, drives us to get up in the morning to tackle tough, often thankless jobs. Many see money as the measure of a man or woman. In the classic movie *Jerry Maguire*, the football star, Cuba Gooding Jr., phones his down-on-his-luck sports agent. He's testing Tom Cruise's commitment. He was thinking of firing him, but now he works up to his pitch, grooving to the blaring beat of his boom box. "It's a very personal, a very important, thing – hell, it's a family motto! Are you ready, Jerry?" Gooding shuts off the music and pauses dramatically. "Show me the money!" he says, and then, to underline the exhortation, cranks up the volume, and springs into a touchdown-like celebratory dance. "Jerry, doesn't it make you feel good just to say that?" coos Gooding. "Just say it to me one time!"

The scene cuts to a defeated Cruise sitting in a crowded office. The sports agent makes a half-heartedly effort. "No," interrupts Gooding, "Show ME the money!" Slowly, the message starts to sink in, Cruise gradually getting louder and louder, until he's screaming, "Show me the money!"

There's a reason the scene is famous, a reason why it's a great parallel for the budding entrepreneur. "Show me the money!" is all about the crazy, irrational, exuberant commitment we need to step out on the ledge. This is what it takes to get results.

The depth and complexity of your relationship to money, commitment and achievement matter. In The Money we explore where and when entrepreneurs face this tension. We return to the pressure cooker of Stanford Launchpad. Time and effort are compressed, driven by the absurd idea that in ten weeks you might actually compete, i.e., launch a new company. Crazy as that sounds, the world is filled with hundreds of accelerators that all bring a nearly identical premise, a promise that in 90 days or less, in the right environment, matched with the right people, practices and assets, a team can build a working prototype, attract early customers, and achieve that all-important market fit. And yes, find the money.

At Stanford, smack in the heart of Silicon Valley, money means so many things. Sand Hill Road, the world's largest concentration of venture capital, is a 30-minute walk from the campus. The headquarters of Google, Facebook, Apple, and dozens of elite firms are less than 15 miles away. Stanford Launchpad can't ignore that reality, and not surprisingly venture capitalists closely monitor each Launchpad cohort. But out in the real, normal world, VCs aren't knocking on most founders' doors. Many must hustle and draw on their networks and friends to crowdfund their way into some initial traction.

Most founders wake up to the harsh reality that they are selling confidence. The world isn't Silicon Valley, overflowing with cash-heavy, risk-taking angel investors. Ambitious founders in cities all over the world discover that to land the big money they must first find their voice. Which brings us to The Pitch.

Why is the pitch so central your journey? Because whether you're an entrepreneur or just hunting a better job or business you often only get one shot. To step up on that stage requires serious courage, because when the spotlight goes on and you've got everyone's attention, you're the only one standing in the way of your own success.

The image of Cuba Gooding, Jr., dancing and shouting, "Show me the money!" is more than a metaphor. You need to be hungry to get the money, and in their own way, each of our characters is fighting for their fair share.

Show me the money.

The Maker
Perry Pushes the Sale

Perry had a candid approach to help prospective Launchpad students understand the money. He spelled it out with dollars and facts: "The average student probably spends $5,000 by the end of the quarter. The average student usually switches their other classes to pass/fail. Oh, and you know, only 40 percent of our students finish the entire program."

Money and competition were right up front. Teams had to rank one another on the first day, and two weeks later upon finishing their initial prototype. Early on, the students got a surprise visit from a dozen top Silicon Valley angels and VCs, each given a fictional $200,000 to invest in the cohort. The investors showed no mercy, most pouring their play cash into a single Launchpad startup. It was Darwinian. Two or three teams grabbed the lion's share. The rest were ignored, or bluntly informed their idea was small or unoriginal.

Competition, voting, feedback, and iterating was constant. Students taped up assignments on whiteboards, the class judging and offering critiques. Perry and Michael brought in potential users to help teams improve their user testing techniques, but most of all, in a dozen different ways, the professors pushed them to sell. Perry, of course, had sold the hard way, on the road like the proverbial traveling salesman, from an SUV stuffed with snowshoes. But selling was often anathema to these privileged Stanford students. Perry pushed them out of their comfort zone. "Sell at least one unit of your product or service by class Monday," was an early, unequivocal assignment. Students had to relentlessly experiment with how they sold, and to whom. An "Inferred Pricing Thermometer" exercise taught them to gauge the difference between "perceived" and "objective" value, and between unit cost and current price, just one of many assignments that reinforced the primacy of selling. Midway into the second week, teams had to: *Focus your product and service on a key feature.... Have a target customer.... Understand that target customer's pain.... Test your pricing.... Iterate your pitch in multiple voices.*

There was an incessant focus on sales and regular feedback loops. Teams dashed off email pitches for a former TV news anchorwoman to simulate how to garner news coverage. An elite Silicon Valley law firm even covered the cost of incorporation – as long as they signed off before the end of the fourth week. This deadline forced teams to accelerate major decisions. Who would be president and CFO? How to share the money? And perhaps most importantly, each team had to make a binding, legal decision on stock ownership. The pressure built to week five, the Beta Test Trade Show, a supercharged evening affair when hundreds of potential investors, corporates, and techies from Silicon Valley and SF poured into Stanford's d.school to cruise the nine team tables and quiz the students on their startups.

Pushing the student teams and their prototypes out there publicly so early offered a dramatic contrast to traditional accelerators that commonly wrapped up their curriculum with a theatrical pitch. That fateful night at the end of April was a thrill for many Launchpad students who suddenly found themselves courted by swarms of potential investors. Yet for a handful of teams this opening night was an abject disappointment.

Perry and Michael gave Launchpad's also-rans a humbling choice: Quit, or essentially repeat the first half of the class. The reason? They hadn't progressed to the stage where they were prepared to accelerate. But survive the Beta Test Trade Show and you were granted another five weeks, a fighting chance to realize your world-changing dream. The second half of the accelerator became even more maniacally focused on selling, reminding them that at the end of the day, it really was all about the money.

The Outsider
Daniel Races Against the Clock

Daniel Lewis and Jon Beekman of Launchpad illuminated a key reality of funding. You might have thought they each sported equal chances of getting funded. Two talented Stanford men with advanced degrees enrolled in the elite accelerator. But their startups couldn't be more different. Daniel was aiming to shake up the legal search world with a revolutionary concept while Beekman was buying potato chips in bulk, and repackaging junk food in wooden crates. The VCs scouting Launchpad ignored Beekman. But by late April it was clear he was winning the most fundamental popularity game of all. Father's Day was approaching, and it dawned on him they might score $30,000 or more on the holiday.

Man Crates was in the money. "We were scrambling, calling our friends, 'We need help putting these things together!'" We didn't know what we were doing, we'd just decided to sell it. Perry and Michael had encouraged us to actually try to sell, so we did. And then it turned into, like, 'Oh my gosh, we're just getting totally crushed.'"

Daniel too was chasing the money, spurred on by Launchpad's clear expectations. Michael Dearing bluntly told the class: "Look, the amount of money you can raise is the amount you can raise in 30 days. If it's taking a lot longer than 30 days, it's not going well." Launchpad Funding Strategy 101 was direct: raise money with energy and high intensity. Exhorted Perry: "Get it done."

The contrast between Beekman's experience and Daniel's was like night and day. Your company type mattered. Beekman couldn't interest a single investor despite the flashing red signs that his revenue-generating web commerce business was an instant hit. Daniel and Nik meanwhile, with no sales, and no expertise in how to build a sophisticated legal search startup, soon had money and investors falling into their lap. On May 1st, at Launchpad's Beta Test Trade Show, a judge from the early rounds of the Stanford business plan competition swung by Daniel and Nik's table for Ravel, their legal search startup. The judge had a unique interest that went beyond his Harvard law degree. He was a VC scouting startups, and he was impressed, having also seen their further progress as a guest mentor in Launchpad. A few days later he phoned them: "Guys, I've seen you through Launchpad, I've seen you through the business plan competition. I'd love for you to come in and talk funding."

This is how easy it was for Daniel. On May 11 they met the VC for cocktails at a bar in Palo Alto. "We sat down and talked it through," said Daniel. "The idea, the existing customers. The big picture." The VC was direct: he wanted a budget. Daniel and Nik cranked out what they'd need on a spreadsheet detailing people, server costs, general overhead, and office space. They shared the $650,000 budget with the VC. "That's great," he said. "Why don't you add a 50 percent buffer to it because it's going to take longer and cost more."

On May 21, the VC asked them to meet his partner at the firm's Palo Alto office, pitch once more, and talk through the increased budget, now about a million. A few hours later, Daniel was shopping for groceries at Trader Joe's when the VC phoned: "Great news. We want to invest. We'll write a check for $500,000, and we'll help you raise the rest of the round."

Timing, competition, and velocity matter for founders and VCs. The very next afternoon, Daniel and Nik were competing in the finals of BASES, the business plan competition, in front of hundreds of investors, business leaders, students and professors. Confident in their chances, after they pitched, they dashed over to attend the day's Launchpad class, which happened to start at 4:15 p.m. But with the award ceremony set to begin less than an hour later, Daniel soon scooted back to see if they might take a prize, and caught a glimpse of a "big goofy check" with Ravel's name written on it. He phoned Nik, telling him to rush back. "Hey, I think we're going to win something here."

It was turning into one pretty awesome day for these two law students who had somehow straddled Launchpad, Stanford's business plan competition, and law school at the very same time, and come out on top. They took second, posed gleefully for a photo op next to their giant check, and ran back to share the win with their Launchpad classmates. Daniel and Nik had landed their first funding, $10,000 in prize money. Oh, and something else. At 5:15 p.m., just as the awards were announced, the VC's term sheet for the half-million-dollar investment in their startup popped into their email boxes.

Twenty-one days and still ticking on Perry's Launchpad 30-day Investment clock. Not a bad start at all.

The Athlete
Joel Taps the Crowd

Joel Heath needed money. He had no job, no readily apparent avenue to fund his speculative venture, and his cash-draining adventure was racking up some serious family costs. Joel and his young son were cruising along Santa Barbara's bucolic, palm tree-lined streets, when they drove by an all-too-familiar sight: a bearded man in scruffy clothes, shuffling along.

The kindergartener put two and two together. "Dad, if Fluid-Stance doesn't work out, will we be homeless?"

The question knocked Joel back. He took a deep breath: "You will never be homeless."

People talk about the risks of a startup, the daily test of commitment. They say it often comes down to guts. "It's not just risk," said Joel. "You want your dad to do anything for you. This was about being vulnerable to my son as a father. And to have that question mark was probably the biggest strain." The five-year-old had good reason to connect his dad's startup to a fear of being homeless. Dad had already explained. These shadowy men had no home because they didn't have a job.

Just like dad.

And while, yes, Joel's family had a home, he had gone all in on his new venue. During five furious weeks in the fall of 2014, Joel visited potential die-casting manufacturers, hired a former colleague for digital marketing, incorporated as Company of Motion, LLC DBA FluidStance, received his first sand cast part, and moved the fledgling operation into a rented garage sandwiched between a tiny strip club and an adult magazine store.

This was getting real: he'd ordered the machine tooling to produce his board at a mind-numbing $100,000 – more than he'd paid for his first house. Serious money. So serious that his hand shook when he wrote the six-figure check. And Joel needed big money now. He wasn't creating an app or software, the sort of startup that scales and more easily attracts investors. Joel hoped to manufacture a complex physical product for which no proven market existed, with all the attendant up-front costs and risks. So far, he'd been able to self-fund all the designers and other independent contractors with his savings, but it would take hundreds of thousands of dollars to produce The Level.

Venture capitalists and angel investors rarely fund such a hard slog, and even if they had expressed interest, Joel probably wouldn't have taken their money. Crowdfunding was how he hoped to leap from prototype to product, and his first paying customers. He saw this as about more than money. Crowdfunding could attract enthusiastic early adopters and give him early eyeballs from the media and the industry, and critical "pre-sale momentum." And so, the Athlete prepared to pour his all into this competition for cash. He'd been practicing classic lean startup principals from the beginning. Incubating his idea in his cottage and garage. Prototyping on the fly. Saving thousands by working with talented, yet inexpensive consultants and experts. But there's an old saying. You have to spend money to make money, and that was doubly true with crowdfunding.

Kickstarter's all-or-nothing model terrified Joel. Fail to reach his sales goal on that popular platform, and he'd have to give all the money back. Indiegogo, based in nearby San Francisco, had no such requirement, and the staff at the smaller platform was willing to talk to him and share best practices as he planned his campaign. Joel teamed up with Todd Widell of Tent, a small creative agency that draws upon contractors or "after hours" talent from bigger agencies. He also hired a former colleague from Deckers, now launching her own digital marketing firm, MAKA.

Joel had settled on a logo. Blind in one eye, he'd become convinced that a one-eyed penguin would be perfect, and had a designer draw it up, and excitedly informed Widell that the image of the playful creature would build off the FluidStance name. "You're kidding me, right?" pushed back a dumbstruck Widell. "You think Herman Miller is going to buy a brand with a penguin as a logo?"

The penguin was out, and soon Joel's investment in his professional image and marketing took hold. The combination of an elegantly designed product geared to a millennial tech audience and excellent pre-Indiegogo press coverage – in *Fast Company, Money*, Trend Hunter and Fox Business – gave him a burst of momentum as they neared the launch.

Joel worked with Tent, MAKA, and the Indiegogo team to craft an authentic campaign, everything from the messaging to the images and videos. The imagery was sleek, the tagline a classic call to action for a board that promised to boost health and productivity: "A shift where you need it most." The campaign trumpeted FluidStance's solid progress the last 18 months on design, engineering, and tooling. And then there was Joel's personal campaign. He just hustled, imploring everybody he knew – family, friends and colleagues – to place their orders the instant the campaign launched. The first 48 hours would be make-or-break.

On January 12, 2015, Joel aimed a camera at himself. He was balancing on a Level by his standing desk in the garage, reggae music blaring in the background. Joel's Indiegogo campaign was about to go live. "All right, here we go!" he said, taking his hands off his desk, and clapping "3-2-1, Go FluidStance" as he hit Enter on his computer, shouting, "Wahoo!"

Within minutes, the orders poured in: $20,000 in sales before sundown, then double his original campaign goal in five days. "Just bliss," recalled Joel, of the showering of affirmation. "Your parents who love you but wonder what the hell you're really doing. A wife understandably tentative on launching a venture. It was validation." And proof of something else, public evidence to his former colleagues that Joel Heath was a fighter with that rare startup founder vision and drive. By March 13, Joel had beaten his original goal eight times over. He'd raised over half a million dollars on Indiegogo.

Now he just had to deliver.

The Evangelist
Uwe Shoots for Startup Perfection

*L**et's build the perfect French startup*, said Uwe to his wife. Uwe was a man who understood timing, influence, and momentum, and he knew that right now startups in France were hot: *It's trendy, it's Emmanuel Macron. It's La France en Marche!* Marketing and sales were stamped into Uwe's character, and he could see plain as day that "as soon as you have a startup everybody looks at you differently." So what if he was old enough to be the father of the typical founder? If ever there was an entrepreneur who could pull off the ideal French startup it was Uwe Diegel.

During the last decade Uwe and his wife Lily had anticipated how the iPhone would revolutionize health care – and jumped on the transformation. Apple opened up the protocol of the phone and gave them the right to register the iHealth brand. "That's where we started," recalled Uwe. "That was in 2009. Suddenly in 2010, all the new magical words started coming out: quantified self, e-health, sustainable health." It was the right approach at the right time. iHealth rode the hot new trend to become a leader in digitally connected blood pressure monitors, glucose monitors, scales and activity trackers.

Charismatic and media savvy, Uwe was a minor celebrity in the eyes of the French tech community. But he was also burned out. iHealth was in many ways run by Chinese factories, and Uwe struggled to elevate the brand. At times he felt he was nothing more than a manufacturer of plastic. "The universe was showing me that I was going in the wrong direction," he said. "I had my mid-life crisis." Uwe had a health scare, left iHealth in the fall of 2016, discovered to his relief that he wasn't going to die, and climbed Mount Kilimanjaro. He told his wife he wanted to "do something meaningful. To look back in five years and say, 'Look what I made.'"

It was time for Uwe to open up his drawer, to answer the all-important question, "What is the right product?" And he had just the thing. More than a decade had passed since his fabulous mini-fridge for transporting temperature sensitive medicines had taken second in NASA's Create the Future Design Contest. Now, he finally had the time, knowhow and sense of purpose to tackle the opportunity. Long ago, he'd registered all kinds of possible names, but Uwe wanted to create a brand and platform for a full product line. They dreamed up 'Lifeina.' The name pronounced itself in any language. "It basically means 'Life in a _____' and then you can build ad infinitum, from "Life in a Box" to "Life In a Tube.""

Through concerted research and prototyping, Uwe cracked the technical riddle that all these years had relegated the device to the drawer. The Peltier Effect was brilliant but unreliable, until with his brother's help he stumbled upon the principle of creating a vacuum to grant the internal thermoelectric elements near-perfect stability, eventually achieving thousands of hours of continuous use in his prototypes. Technology solved, Uwe set out to embrace French socialist thinking, to "make this perfect company where nobody has more responsibility than anybody else." He found four bright youths, an international cadre – French, British, and South African – all living and working in Paris. There would be no hierarchy, no boss – a radical experiment in how to build a startup. "I said, 'All right, you're starting the business. I'll put up the money. Nobody gets paid until the product is on the market, and then we divide the business in fifths.'"

Uwe was invited to pitch Lifeina at Credit Agricole's tech incubator Le Village, and the director promptly invited him to join the next cohort. The dream was taking shape. The team posed for Le Village pics, and everyone loved the energy and ambiance at the bustling hive in the center of Paris. Every Friday at the Diegel flat near the Place de l'Opéra, Lily would whip up her fabulous dumplings to go with the pizza, beer and brainstorming. The first few meetings were fantastic. That is until Uwe soon found "that if you don't actually push people and give them a salary the work doesn't get done."

They needed the money, and Uwe knew just how they could get it. With three recent successful crowdfunding campaigns under his belt, he thought, "No problem. We'll crowdfund Lifeina." Uwe designed a perfect campaign. He shot beautiful videos, built a community of 7,500 Facebook followers, and crafted gorgeous samples by hand.

They launched in June of 2017 – and nothing happened. Stunned, Uwe individually emailed the 7,500 people on Facebook who had indicated interest, asking, "Can you tell us why you're not buying?" He read all 700 replies and quickly saw that nearly everyone said the same thing: *Mr. Diegel, we love LifeinaBox. We will buy it. The moment it's out we will be the first customer. But we suffer from a chronic disease, and we suffer every day, continuously.*

Translation: They weren't going to spend real money on something that wouldn't be available for another six months. Uwe did not sulk. He analyzed nearly every single product campaign on Indiegogo and Kickstarter and discovered that "there had never been one for chronic disease that worked." Gadgets and toys sold. A serious product for a chronic disease? Never. It was back to square one. Uwe's grand French egalitarian experiment was going nowhere. Maybe it was time to put Lifeina back in the box?

Something needed to change if this startup was going to make it. Nothing was happening in Paris, so Uwe decided to expand his horizon, to gain some ground on his search for traction. That fall, Europe's biggest tech conference would be held in Lisbon, just a two-hour plane ride southwest. Uwe decided to go. On a whim. Alone.

He'd heard that Web Summit had a big startup contest.

The Guardian

Karoli Runs for Money

Standing on the deck of the green Tallink Superstar ferry as she neared the Helsinki harbor, Karoli felt that her Jobbatical startup dream was running out of time. The boat was uncharacteristically late, and as she eyed the crowded port she feared the investor she was scheduled to meet wouldn't wait, that she'd blown her chance.

Karoli always threw herself into new challenges with the assumption that she'd find a way, but raising money was proving to be harder than she'd imagined. She'd had high hopes for her first pitch to the Estonian Business Angels Network but had failed to anticipate two fundamental facts. The angels were all men, and regardless of her success as a young entrepreneur and TV executive she was still most definitely a woman, and Estonian men almost never funded startups led by women. Not only that, but she was a young mother suddenly stepping back out onto the stage before a brutal audience – 40 stony faced men in suits. "I had come back after being at home with a child for a year, which kind of takes down the confidence, and then suddenly, you're the only woman in front of all those men." Her pitch had not gone well. The president of EstBAN unsettled her with the lone question, clearly dismissive of her startup's potential. None of the Estonian angels wanted to invest. Not a single one offered a word of encouragement. After the pitches, Karoli's heart sank as the angels crowded around all the male founders, leaving her completely alone. "I did think that was the place where I felt really small."

Was she really the right person to execute this vision? She hadn't worked in over a year. Her teenage entrepreneurial success was a distant memory. The truth was that she was a novice in both tech and the recruitment industry. To stand a chance, she had to gather herself and rediscover her strength. Gradually, she began going on long, invigorating runs, a pastime that always grounded her and boosted her confidence. She steeled herself and applied to pitch another group she hoped might be more receptive, FiBAN, the Finnish Business Angels Network. "I actually had to work quite a bit," she recalled. "Because if you're starting something you need to commit to yourself that you believe and that this will change something."

Most of all Karoli had to overcome her own self-doubts that June morning as the ferry neared Helsinki, with what to her mind might be her last chance. Her pitch to the Finnish investors had gone surprisingly well. Three investors expressed interest, but in the end, only one agreed to a meeting. And now she feared she might lose him too. "The ferry was twenty minutes late, which meant that I'm late for my meeting with the only investor that agreed to meet with me." It was June, the weather warm, Karoli wearing a blue dress, stockings and her favorite high-heeled blue boots set off by girl-ish yellow bows. "I thought, 'Okay, well, I'm late, should I take a cab?' Then I saw the port was completely jammed, so taking a cab wouldn't save any time."

The boat docked, and Karoli broke into a run, and then after a few hundred yards realized, *I have to get to the meeting faster!* She skipped to a half stop, slipped off her boots, and raced through the crowd in her stockings. Two straight miles pounding her feet down the streets of Helsinki. She arrived at the hotel just in time to meet Jan Boethius, the man she hoped would be her angel.

"I'm sweating, and it's not because of you," she bravely announced, catching her breath as she explained her mad dash. They talked for two hours, and he closed with words she'd never forget: "I don't have any idea about this industry, but I believe in you!"

Karoli had her first investor, a Finn, merely a single angel. Her confidence rising, she became even more locked in on raising her first round. Soon after her Helsinki run a Singularity contact introduced her via email to Christopher Sier, a British businessman connected to the university. "I was told that we should meet because somebody had told Chris great things about me," she recalled. But Karoli was a disciplined, intensely focused founder, adept at saying "no" to extraneous meetings or activities. *I don't have time for you,* she thought to herself, *I'm fundraising.* After mulling it over, Karoli reluctantly met with Sier in Tallinn, all the while knowing she should be elsewhere. Only near the end of their talk did she mention that she was hunting angels.

"I would like to invest," Sier said abruptly. Not maybe. Not a question. A firm declaration. It was the last thing Karoli had expected. She did her best to appear nonplussed, nodded "OK" and made a mental note to herself: *Never underestimate the people we meet.*

That was July of 2014. Two investors on board, Karoli was gaining momentum. "Now I had UK and Finnish investors, so it got a little more interesting for Estonian angels." Sure enough, an early stage Estonian fund ended up joining the round. All told, Karoli won commitments from angels and investors from five different countries, demonstrating her strength and initiative in looking beyond tiny Estonia for money – Finland, UK, Estonia, Latvia and Russia.

That summer her brother quit his online media product manager job, and joined as another co-founder. Jobbatical was on track with $340,000 in investor commitments, a solid showing for an Estonian startup. Karoli expected the round to close by the end of August, which turned out to be another rookie assumption. The bills piled up. Now she was paying for two salaries, her bank account dipping toward zero. September came and went, and still the investor money had yet to arrive. Tired of shuttling between cafés, she'd rented her team a shoe box office. It was dusty and cramped and Karoli thought the building might have asbestos but they were so happy to finally have an office. The funding would close any day.

It didn't. Karoli had spent all her money. Her two co-founders had left their day jobs to follow her vision. She fretted. Had she led them astray? When the angels made their financial commitments she had imagined the process would be quick. "But then it turned out to be a contractual disaster." So nervous that she couldn't sleep, running out of savings, unsure whether she should or could get a business loan to get by, she found herself thinking, "What the hell am I doing here?"

Karoli prepared for the worst. A couple more weeks of delays, and she'd have to file for bankruptcy. And then when she began to fear it was all for naught, when it was truly down to the wire, late that October, Karoli Hindriks closed her $340K round, and became just the second woman in Estonia to receive startup funding. The Guardian was back on track. Jobbatical, a startup all about helping people to work in the place of their dreams, was in business.

The Accidental

Mait Finds His Voice

Mait Müntel was preparing to take Lingvist to Techstars. Famous for grooming startups to attract funding, the accelerator was all about the money. The erstwhile scientist wondered. Did he really need help in this area?

He was itching to focus on the highly complex task of designing Lingvist algorithms and software, and to his mind the million-plus euros he'd raised would keep them in the money for years. But momentum won out, and Mait and a handful of Lingvist developers moved into a London Airbnb in the spring of 2014, and dove into the intensive three-month program. Mentor madness was how Mait described it. "So many people packed into one room that you cannot even hear the person next to you who's trying to mentor you." Mait's brain was pulled like taffy in different directions, as he struggled to untangle what often seemed like conflicting advice. Then came the fast-paced mini-MBA-style courses and lectures. Mait knew nothing about business. He was suffering from information overload.

Time management was not a skill he'd learned as a particle physicist. He was a novice founder. "So I jumped between these mentor meetings and coding, which are two very different things," he said. The latter required deep focus, while the mentoring and course curriculum shifted from "one person to another, from one topic to another." Mait feared he was doing both badly. Building machine learning software was no trivial task.

Worst of all, he had to learn how to pitch investors. He'd had a stroke of beginner's luck on the big stage at Slush. At Techstars, as the stakes increased and the pressure mounted, pitching was becoming his Achilles heel. Each founder gave an introductory speech, and Mait was "the last and the worst." He knew how ridiculous it was, this erstwhile scientist promising "to teach you how to speak languages, and you cannot speak yourself, and you have this awful Estonian accent, and you are not convincing anybody."

Techstars knew many founders struggled with stage fright, and right in the heart of London they had the perfect remedy. They took them out to the legendary Speakers' Corner in Hyde Park, where for centuries, politicians and all manner of orators had stood before the crowds and barked out their speeches to hostile audiences. So Mait headed out to Speakers' Corner, accompanied often by Ott, who had quit his job to join the team. Mait had sheepishly suggested Ott or someone else could do the pitch, but his co-founder wasn't going to let him off the hook. Mait had to do this. "Then we were in the park. I pitched him, and he listened," said Mait. "It was very painful, but he didn't lose hope."

Mait took to the Techstars stage, one final trial before the big Demo Day. Thirty people in the room, Ott watching intently. Mid-pitch the stocky, 200-pound-man did something inexplicable. "I literally collapsed on the stage. Yes, it's extremely embarrassing because everybody is looking at you," recalled Mait. "You see that nobody believes in you. How can you pitch the next day?"

The Accidental had reached a desultory low point. There were so many things he didn't anticipate or understand on this unexpected journey of entrepreneurship. But this was so…humiliating. Could he recover? Even the Techstars mentors were alarmed, and suggested Mait might be a lost cause. Perhaps Lingvist could find an actor? Dream up some other solution? But Mait knew that wouldn't work. He pulled himself together, and returned to Speakers' Corner to "scream it alone." He practiced his pitch all day and late into the night. Fail on this big stage, and he would let everyone down. Mait was pitching to his team, and their future. Who would join or invest in a company with a founder who collapsed during a pitch?

The head of Techstars' Berlin office gave Mait a pivotal last-minute tip. Identify your strongest slide, and move it to the third position. The following day at Whitechapel Theatre, an old music hall turned arthouse movie theatre in the East End, Techstars presented its London Demo Day. Before a packed 500-strong house of tech media, angels and VCs, Mait felt a surge of adrenaline, found his words and dialed into a "super-focused mental state." Reporters were impressed, both by the particle physicist, and by his ambitious goal of taking a big chunk of the $58 billion language learning market. TechCrunch repeated Mait's key line in its story, "Every moment spent learning is turned into a valuable insight," and seemed to view the company as the cream of the crop: "With the focus for large tech companies like Google, Apple and others on machine learning, I feel that this is one to watch for its talent alone, whether it gets applied to language learning or something completely different down the line."

Mait had found his voice just in time. He'd nailed his pitch, earned the respect of his team and attracted critical media interest. He couldn't know at this moment how important this would prove. They were all exhausted, and upon returning to Tallinn, took a well-deserved break. But it wasn't long before Mait realized that though their million-euros-plus investment round had finally hit their Estonian bank, everything in this startup world cost more than he imagined. Lingvist was playing a long game, aiming to build something serious and deeply technical in a crowded language-learning tech market, goals that would require money, lots of money. But Mait was no longer worried. Overcoming his stage fright to pull off a critical performance at Techstars had steeled his nerve, and delivered a critical data point. Whatever he had to do next – attract more funding, find more customers, figure out the tech – maybe, just maybe, he had what it took to get the Money.

The Leader

Allan Builds His Runway

Allan learned to his excitement that Twitter was moving into the 1355 Market tower, and he leapt at the opportunity to acquire a lease. He saw it as a chance to "hitch a ride on a bigger whale." Being in the Twitter tower, "being part of this watering hole" would help catalyze the community he wanted to gather around him, this new kind of tech incubator. This bold venture would require some serious upfront cash. The buildout would cost roughly a million, the lease about $100,000 a month. Amazingly Allan funded the effort simply through his reputation and tight network of colleagues and friends, a testament to his independent, entrepreneurial mojo. "There was no one big investor," said Allan. "We raised money from small investors." He was confident. He'd calculated that they'd break even at 60 percent of capacity.

Creating culture, attitude, atmosphere and action was his goal, and part of his inspiration had come from all the other incubators he'd visited. "I felt that RocketSpace and Plug and Play were such horrible shells," he recalled of two other prominent destinations at the time. "I found them all to be disappointing. The small ones particularly. They felt to me like shared offices, not really incubators." Allan noticed an absence of interaction and sharing. Lots of private offices with closed doors. "I wanted to design a space where there was not one private office," he explained. "Take an extreme view. This wouldn't work for everybody. You don't have your own room, the work environment is wide open. The concept was that you'd share ideas, knowledge, and lessons learned."

Allan called it Runway, a name both literal and metaphoric, chosen to convey the long, rectangular space and the ramp he hoped to create to launch great new ideas. Unlike the ill-fated WeWork, the bloated global real estate play, where workers crowd into tiny glass aquarium-like caged offices with minimal public space, Allan designed his incubator so that about 50 percent was "wide open." You entered the Twitter building at 1355 Market, took the elevator to the 10th floor, and entered Runway, a broad open hall nearly the length of a football field, adjoining rows of long worktables next to windows. At the end looking out at City Hall, lay an expansive event space. Runway boasted a large, open kitchen, a comfortable lounge area, surrounded by small meeting rooms and phone booths, and one of Allan's fanciful touches, the coolest meeting space of all, an igloo. The open space was nearly equal in size to the workspace, what Allan termed the golden ratio. "If you were a member of Runway, you couldn't get to your desk without bumping into someone," he recalled. "If you were social enough, inevitably you'd share ideas. That's the magic. With all these open spaces we created collisions – accidental collisions."

Allan took a contrarian approach to promoting his fledgling incubator. He never spent a dollar on Google ads or traditional advertising or marketing. He wanted to practice a technique "that Seth [Godin] was a big proponent of, which is word of mouth." Allan growth-hacked, reaching out to his network and beyond for hosting events at Runway. "We didn't charge the event producers or organizers at all for using our venue space and that brought in a ton of companies and people and they would ask, 'What's this?'" Allan hired young startup enthusiasts to run the space and manage the bookings, building a culture of "people who are genuinely interested in entrepreneurship." There was no "upstairs, downstairs" hierarchy of private offices. No stratification and lots of serendipity. "You had companies that were referring each other to investors. You'd talk to your fellow startup down the hall, and you might say, 'I've been looking for a great CTO or something,' and someone says, 'My friend is leaving Google and might be a great candidate.'"

As the saying goes, if you build it, they will come. Runway was soon bustling with 80 startups, more than a few founders skateboarding or scootering up and down the long broad hall. Allan was helping to lead this movement in San Francisco without even realizing it was happening all over the world. People just like him, independent entrepreneurs with drive and vision, were launching incubators like Rockstart in Amsterdam, Beta-i in Lisbon, Lift99 in Tallinn, Schoolab in Paris. More would follow in San Francisco: Galvanize, The Vault, Founders Space. Within six months of opening in January of 2013, Runway was full, boasting over 200 people, and Allan was learning, engaging with this new community he'd created, helping many of the early teams to attract investors and customers. Four exited in the first three years, with one, the drone firm Skycatch, attracting capital from Google Ventures, and $47 million in investment.

Allan's Runway was cleared for take-off.

The Conductor
Carlos Finds His Spark

Carlos Muela was ready to fill his second canvas. SoMa StrEat Food Park was now a proven new model with tremendous potential. It had been a bold move. Carlos and his family had fronted all the cash for the park with their own savings. No loans. No outside investors. A quarter of a million dollars, a huge gamble for a small business. And yet the bet had paid off spectacularly. For the last two and half years, the park had been packed. Carlos was a different guy now. Twenty-seven years old. A success story. A man with this close, trusted relationship with nearly two hundred San Francisco Bay Area food trucks.

In early 2015 Laura Tepper reached out to Carlos with the promise of a 16,000-square-foot blank canvas she needed to fill. The project manager with the Mission Bay Development Group wanted to talk food trucks. Carlos had scouted the area years before and understood its promise. Mission Bay was a booming new southward expansion of San Francisco, a product of the furious growth of tech and biotech. Sandwiched between China Basin, AT&T Park and the Dogpatch neighborhood, Mission Bay was the site of UCSF's gleaming new hospital, numerous corporate pharmaceutical offices, major new buildings for Uber and Cisco, multimillion-dollar condos and the designated site of the Warriors' soon-to-be-built new stadium. It was about to become a very hot zone.

Tepper faced the classic chicken-and-egg dilemma that confounds development agencies. Mission Bay was a massive, multi-year project with distinct stages. Tepper's role was to come up with creative ways to fill out the interstitial spaces, the unused parcels of land that weren't slotted to be anything for years. Though some might eventually become public parks, that was far off in the future. "They had a soccer field and a garden," said Carlos. "But it was still nothing.

It wasn't the spark that the neighborhood needed."

There was a gap at Mission Bay, a fundamental absence of places to eat, drink or hang out, the core elements that a community needs to thrive. Tepper gave Carlos a tour of the empty parcel on 4th Street near the medical center. You needed vision to understand. The barren space was surrounded by construction sites. The condos weren't finished. But Tepper believed in Carlos, and made her pitch. "We have no food, we have no drinks," she told him. "Something like SoMa StrEat Food Park would be incredible down here. This is exactly what we want, and you're the guy to do it."

As she described the development agency's ambitious plans, Carlos put on his best poker face. He didn't want to look eager, but he was counting the money. Calculating the thousands of hospital and corporate workers who would need to eat lunch. Knowing that "they were not going to have restaurants" in the neighborhood for several years. Imagining all those new local condo owners who would soon be itching for nearby dinner options. The Conductor sensed the potential synergy with his existing SoMa StrEat Food Park just a mile away, where business was bursting at the seams. He had his own demand to fill. "I had a big list of food trucks and nowhere to put them."

Carlos also weighed the risks. San Francisco had thrown obstacles in front of his first park at every turn. "I never wanted to do it again," he said. "Which is sad, right? They just burned me. I got so burned out that I didn't want to ever do anything again in the city. I said no to other opportunities, but when Laura called it was just the right time." Here, he was being courted. Instead of *Push* it was *Pull*. Success begets success. Carlos had "good money in the bank," and he was ready to take on something new. And as he continued to meet with Tepper it became clear that the redevelopment agency was willing to invest the up-front capital to help build out the park.

Tepper too was something of a visionary. Orchestrating a major new, complex development in San Francisco would be an entrepreneurial process. It couldn't happen all at once. As they iterated, lean-startup style, she had a breakthrough idea for a name: Parklab. Quite literally experimental parks – athletic fields, community gardens, and now in the planning stages, Carlos Muela's latest food truck extravaganza. He had ideas about how to bring fire and light and energy to this empty lot. He was beginning to fathom the scale of what was happening, the budding creative and financial potential. Carlos was becoming a producer and choreographer, growing more comfortable with his identity as a Conductor. He had one thriving San Francisco food truck platform and was about to build another, and they were connected and symbiotic.

Carlos had a name too for his second San Francisco food truck startup. He called it Spark.

The Collaborator
Joe Makes the French Connection

Nestled in the French countryside near Chantilly, in a 19th century chateau built by the Rothschild family, Joe Boggio sat surrounded by Team One, 150 executives in finely tailored European suits, all tuned in to hear this bold plan to spread innovation throughout the firm. Joe had most definitely left Microsoft. This was Capgemini, the giant French IT company, his new employer, and Joe had more than a little interest in the proceedings. He was sitting in the front row, staring at the presentation he'd helped build, watching Lanny Cohen, Capgemini's Chief Technology Officer, deliver their pitch. They wanted money. Millions of euros to design and build a thriving innovation hub thousands of miles away in San Francisco.

Joe had come a long away from his one-stoplight town in the Midwest. A long way from Microsoft. Corporate intrapreneurs take chances too. On new projects. New jobs. This is how it happened for Joe. He partnered with Capgemini on a project. The 125,000-employee French firm liked his work, and promptly made him an offer. Joe accepted, but soon wondered if he'd made a mistake. The job boxed him into what felt too much like a sales position. So Joe improvised, exercising his new skills in fostering corporate collaboration, choreographing a power dinner between Lanny Cohen, then the divisional CEO of Capgemini and one of 3M's leading executives. The dinner was a success. Shortly afterward, Lanny was charged with setting the company's overall innovation agenda and strategy. He reached out to Joe. "You know this stuff, and I see that you can organize yourself around these subjects," Lanny told him. "Would you like to partner with me to create our company's response?"

The two dove in feet-first, starting with an internal scan of Capgemini's ongoing innovation efforts. They identified 33 innovation centers in eight countries. No two alike. No common process, training, or roles. They ranged from a loosely funded "room" with some signage, all the way to thirty- to forty-person labs that did sophisticated prototyping. "We had very inconsistent branding, resourcing, funding, prototyping and metrics," recalled Joe. But there were huge strengths. Capgemini had experience from fashion to aerospace, business transformation and technology deployment. They were truly global. "We had a strong community and culture of people who had a high affinity towards innovation," said Joe, and both he and Lanny knew that this shift was absolutely critical. The life span of the typical company on the S&P 500 was dipping to 15 years, a terminal trend when you considered that Capgemini's largest clients had on average been in business for almost a century. "Our clients are Volkswagen and BMW," recalled Joe. "And damn, here comes Tesla, what are they gonna do?"

To find the answer, they scoured the competitive landscape, touring dozens of innovation centers and labs in Silicon Valley. They visited the legendary PARC in Palo Alto, and a host of corporate labs or briefing centers, from SAP to Cisco, Walmart, and Orange. They saw that rubbing shoulders with startups was key to most successful new corporate innovation labs. Joe and Lanny could spot the pretenders. They seemed like "museums, theaters or showcases." In contrast, the best centers were "places where collaboration took place – co-innovation, co-location," recounted Lanny. "A startup and a corporate partner. Bringing all the expertise necessary to create engagements in experiential environments." As the duo toured the brand-new tech incubators taking hold in San Francisco, they could see the value of the quickened pace. The unbridled collaboration and acceleration that comes when diverse teams gel in creative environments.

There was no time to waste. Joe pulled together a statistic that showed Capgemini's key competitors had poured a billion into venture funds and innovation labs in the last year. "There was an incredible amount of activity in the innovation space," said Joe. "But

everything was formative. Nobody had really gotten this right yet."
Joe and Lanny started whiteboarding. The concepts and words were
clunky at first, but Joe wasn't going to repeat his earlier Microsoft
blunder. They tested their early prototype with key Capgemini
business unit leaders, and major clients – "we'd tweak and tune and
calibrate it" – refining it over several weeks to what they hoped
would be the essence of this new innovation hub for clients visiting
the world's tech mecca.

The vision would require a major investment in the pricey Bay
Area. "Very senior people at Capgemini were saying, 'You'll never
get funding for that. Not in our culture,'" said Joe. "But we pushed
back to say that this would not be an innovation center" in the classic
sense. They envisioned it as more fundamental, a "mechanism" and
a distinct place "to explore future business models and culture for
the entire company."

Joe, Lanny, and a colleague had holed up at Lanny's house on
the Jersey shore the weekend before the Team One chateau pitch
and built the final presentation together, before jetting off to
Paris. It was a big leap of imagination. This wasn't going to be a
showroom or a lab, but a place to exchange ideas, a place to take
tangible steps into the future, and so it would be called Capgemini's
Applied Innovation Exchange. The concept sounded simple and
direct. They would host major clients coming to the Valley for an
innovation immersion. Help them tour the area. Not just visits to the
tech giants, but deep engagements with the up-and-coming startups,
and meetings with the nimbler corporates. The goal was to learn
to deploy startup expertise in pilots, to create new solutions from
within. The "Exchange" was about focusing on business challenges,
demonstrating how innovation was being "Applied" for successful
outcomes.

Cohen began his pitch by playing a video that Joe had stitched
together on his laptop, a playful collage of early fun interviews with
Jeff Bezos, Steve Ballmer, Mark Zuckerberg and other leaders, a
snapshot of the sudden rise of digital innovations. Another slide

detailed the hundreds of millions of dollars competitors were already spending on innovation annually, and the billions being spent by their own clients. Another represented the over 250 innovation labs already built in Silicon Valley. This was a pitch for corporate cash, seed funding for a project. It happens every day in boardrooms around the globe.

Lanny and Joe followed up their powerful presentation with one-on-one meetings with all of Capgemini's key business unit leaders, and closed the sale. They won executive approval to build out an innovation center for an 8,000-square-foot space, a commitment with a several-year lease of millions of dollars. It was September of 2014, and they had an ambitious goal of opening before the end of the year. They'd gotten the company's buy-in. But it's one thing to win the pitch, quite another to close the deal. They knew that the vast majority of corporate innovation centers were failures. Money didn't guarantee success. Real estate in San Francisco was red hot. Tech firms, startups and, yes, corporates were grabbing every possible office space and storefront in the city they could find. Lanny and Joe had to hunt for the right location, make an offer, and close that deal.

They had the money. Now they had to find the perfect place.

The Visionary
Risto Rocks Palo Alto

Risto had wriggled out of the box that was Finland. He'd traded Helsinki for California. For Palo Alto, where Risto decided that his company had to have "a nice wooden house." A house that would become more than a house. Finns are homebodies, in part because of the long, harsh winters. It's tradition too. The home is the center of family and community in Finland. Beyond these cultural reasons for wanting a house for his freshly transplanted company, Risto was pursuing a vision. Idean was about design: the house would celebrate the essence of his company. First for his team, and then for the larger UX design movement he hoped to lead. "If you stay eight, nine hours a day at work, why not spend it in a great environment?" he recalled. "I thought if I rented a home with a nice, big backyard, we could also host parties. Bring clients. Start making our name."

Risto found that perfect wooden house on Kipling Street in downtown Palo Alto. The rent was $10,000 a month, $120,000 a year, with a ten-year lease that with rent increases required a long-term commitment of $1.5 million. It seemed an extravagant expenditure for the small company. Yet Pohjola, the chairman of his board, had his back. He pushed him to take the lease, telling him he thought it was a smart idea. Risto signed the lease, and almost instantly, the house became foundational. "It was like a filter," said Risto. "If you don't like this environment you're not going to like Idean. If you do, you'll have a frickin' good time with us – clients and employees."

Companies, like people, need to assert their identity. Dream. Stake out who they are, and what they want. The house became Idean's new Californian identity, in an iconic location close enough to the original Apple store that each fall when new iPhones came out the massive line of Apple enthusiasts would snake around the block past Risto's front door. The team painted the house together, light silvery blue on the outside. Risto's wife did the tasteful interiors, including the write-on whiteboard walls, lending it a comfortable, homey, yet professional feel. Just after summer, Risto decided what they really needed was a party. This was atypical for Palo Alto. The town may be notable for many things, but night life is not one of them, and Risto was about to shake things up in the neighborhood. He had a saying: "We are in the business of making friends." To his mind, the best way to make friends was to throw a party.

These weren't tepid, corporate beer-and-chips afterthoughts in stale Silicon Valley offices. They were wild, elbow-to-elbow, two- to three-hundred-person packed blowouts crowded into "that frickin' backyard," so wild that the cops were often called around midnight. But there was a method to the madness. "It was good for team spirit and culture," said Risto. "It enabled us to get our clients to come to our place, not the other way around. We were like, 'Hey, we're going to be throwing this party, please come on over, you're welcome!'"

Risto saw the parties as a fun excuse to show off that they were a design firm. "Every single time we had a theme, like Black and White, or Fifties or Midsummer's Night, or Chinese New Year. This was of course marketing, in a way, to design an experience. Not to put an advertisement somewhere, but to provide an emotional connection." Just as the house was more than a house, the parties became more than parties. Around the same time, Risto did something else remarkable. He put on his first UX Summit, attracting top firms like Google, Netflix, HP and Intel for a packed 200-person one day affair titled, *Brand is Dead, UX is the New Brand*. He'd never done anything like this before. "The playbook for that was like, I go and invite a bunch of my new friends, new clients, or people I'd like to work with as the speakers," said Risto. The UX Summit was a design party that instantly established Risto and his upstart company's leadership. They didn't promote Idean: "We focused on the theme and the speakers, providing value to the audience, and vice versa."

It's hard to understate how remarkable this was. Not just Risto planting his Finnish flag, but staking out territory in the Valley. Less than two years earlier, this head of a small, struggling studio had begun his monthly California forays, holing up for a couple of weeks at a time at the Sheraton in Palo Alto, masquerading as a local. It was a crazy experiment, a sudden quantum leap. By all rights this UX Summit should have been masterminded by IDEO, the far larger, established Silicon Valley design giant. But that would have belied the reality that this was about ambition, risk-taking, and vision. Risto was acting like the head of a much larger firm with the boldness and money to do big things.

Risto's party was just getting started.

Takeaways:
Landing the Money

Money makes the world go round. Scoring investment and backing requires confidence. And a great pitch. What Faces help bring in the Money?

Makers speed the investment cycle.
Outsiders travel multiple paths to the money.
Guardians convert investors to their cause.
Athletes put it all on the line.
Accidentals don't plan for the money.
Conductors attract platform backers.
Collaborators master the supporting role.
Visionaries invest in their future.
Evangelists embrace selling.
Leaders turn to their tribe for the money.

The Test

Mait, a man who knew more about physics than 99.99999 percent of the world, was discovering fast that he knew next to nothing about startups.

Welcome to The Test. You've reached the pivotal trial of your idea, product or project. The gut-check. Battle-tested entrepreneurs live for this stage. The thrill and high stakes of The Test are why when they do finally succeed – even after failing two or three times – they're often hungry to come back for more.

What does it take? An ability to leap obstacles with tenacity and courage – to push beyond your comfort zone. The Test is also about speed. Suddenly you're that Athlete thrust into a vastly more competitive arena where everything happens faster, where there's no time to think, barely time to do. And that heightened pressure demands another level of commitment. The Test is where our characters learn to fully trust their nature. Take our Guardian. She may seem outmatched by greater bureaucratic powers, but her deep sense of purpose and mission help her tap exactly what she needs to navigate this perilous path.

The Test is about ambition, reaching higher than you thought possible. And tenacity. Our Visionary knows that in the world of UX design he is viewed as no more than an ant, but he dares to dance with the elephants, to take an extraordinary gamble in competing for a massive, multimillion-dollar contract. The Test is ultimately about making your own luck. This is not just about spotting a rising wave, but throwing caution to the wind, and jumping on board no matter how wild the ride.

Entrepreneurs going through this stage need an indomitable mindset. Stuff often goes horribly wrong during the Test. Two of our ten characters dealt with near business-death experiences. Full-blown disasters, the sort that can sink a product launch. Others desperately need to notch sales or garner more funding to keep the doors open, while one faces a life challenge that makes business seem trivial. And yet many thrive quite simply because so much is on the line. Our Outsider is uncannily prepared for the curve balls thrown his way by investors and the daunting challenge of securing premium content for his prototype before running short of cash. The Test is the time to improvise, to troubleshoot, as our Athlete must do in ways he couldn't have imagined.

The stakes are do-or-die, and the Evangelist, picking himself up after a humiliating failure, knows that his pitch ultimately will not be about technology and market size but capturing hearts on the big stage. Finally, there's Mait Müntel, our Accidental. Mistake prone. Oblivious to how many new things he must do at one time. Yet indomitable. A man who is learning to pull on his pants while running out the door. A man who takes a long, calculated shot to fly halfway around the world for one last chance to continue the dream.

The Maker
Perry Sets the Pace

Launchpad was like *Survivor* for entrepreneurs. Conflict and drama were both expected and exploited for the greater good. Teams bonded, teams splintered. Whatever happened, Perry and Michael mined the real-life frictions of starting a business as powerful lessons for the whole cohort. One day, for instance, a student announced he wouldn't continue on with his team after the semester because he wasn't ready to throw himself behind what was fast becoming a real business. "One of your peers is standing up and having a whole discussion about how somebody's leaving because it's a real company," said Perry. "Because they actually need to get space, sign leases, distribute stock. It's like, 'We've got to get going!'"

Launchpad accelerated that forward lean, keeping the students on their toes, thrusting them out of their comfort zones. Some days they were spontaneously tested on their ability to hustle. They walked into the classroom to find Perry and Michael unveiling a cache of plastic cups, ice, pitchers, and drink mix – all the ingredients for a pop-competition to sell the most lemonade. The classic childhood summer pastime might seem a silly diversion. But Launchpad's Lemonade Sales Day celebrated ingenuity and salesmanship. This was a winner-take-all contest. No rules, just an exhortation to sell like crazy, and over the years the best teams showed moxie. One squad announced they were raising money for female entrepreneurs, and collected $400 in less than an hour. Another gave impromptu campus tours to visitors, charging for the service and offering the lemonade as a freebie, raking in a stunning $700. The next year two squads vied for the top spot. One team caffeinated their lemonade and sold it door to door in the dorms as a morning coffee alternative, collecting $656. Impressive, but not that year's winner. The other team, shut down by a bureaucrat who said they couldn't sell on campus, improvised by soliciting "donations" for their startup. They cleared over $2,000, which combined with their classmates' sales, nearly topped $4,000 for one hour's work.

The exuberance and can-do spirit of Lemonade Sales Day provided a critical lesson. Teams almost always earned more selling lemonade than they had so far in selling their own fledgling product. What did that teach? That startups needed to sell a whole lot better. Perry had just the remedy. Soon after the mid-semester Beta Test Trade Show, Perry confronted them with the 10X Sales Challenge, where the goal was to scale and sell ten times more than they'd managed to date. It sounded impossible, but the test often inspired exponential leaps.

Growth was about more than sales. Hiring and managing were also critical startup skills. So, during the second five weeks, each team was assigned a few freshmen interns. Most teams passively directed their recruits to a shared Google Drive document, with feeble results. The best teams met the enthusiastic youngsters in person, discerned their passions, and channeled those interests and talents toward essential tasks, often in the process grooming their first hires.

Launchpad inspired the students to throw enormous effort and ambition behind highly practical company building techniques. Perry and Michael didn't pre-judge success. This crash course in the Maker mindset was about imprinting the founders and teams with a direct, action-focused way of doing and making. The professors were forging a method, just as more than a hundred years ago a Harvard professor pioneered the case method of teaching law. The secret was going beyond studying, in casting off the shackles of your academic training.

Launchpad was about making stuff, selling stuff. Getting results. Perry and Michael were teaching a method and mindset.

It wasn't just about launching. The question was whether you had what it took to keep the momentum after you got out there.

The Outsider
Daniel Goes to Harvard

Daniel Lewis awoke one June morning to find his email inbox filled with half a dozen introductions to legendary Sand Hill Road venture capitalists, from Peter Thiel to Andreessen Horowitz. "We have signed a term sheet to invest in Ravel's seed round. This is an eight-billion-dollar-plus industry owned by two companies," read the effusive email from New Enterprise Associates, which was backing them to the tune of half a million dollars. "It's practically begging to be toppled, and to date no one has even attempted it. We are looking to fill out the syndicate; co-founders Daniel Lewis and Nik Reed are talking to all the other top-tier firms."

Daniel and Nik settled into a rhythm that summer. Studying each morning for the bar exam, pitching elite venture firms most afternoons, back to the books in the evening. The studying was straightforward. As for the pitching, they had to be ready for a few curve balls. They rarely got past the first few slides before being interrupted by a blunt question as to why the upstarts wouldn't be slaughtered by the duopoly of LexisNexis and Westlaw. Daniel and Nik could soon anticipate the queries and rejections. Like the common "you're not a good fit" brush-off. Or the cavalier put-down: "You know, it's not a product that I can take home and show my family." They had to learn not to take these digs too personally.

They also learned to begin with confidence. Recalled Daniel: "We'd tee it up and let them know if there was a general counsel at the venture fund, it might be a good idea to have them join in." The positive attitude worked. North Bridge Venture Partners liked the pitch and the co-founders and invested $500,000. On top of the initial $500,000 from New Enterprise (and a few smaller contributions from others), this brought the first round to approximately $1.1 million.

The money cleared their bank a few days before they each took – and passed – the bar exam. Michael Dearing of Launchpad let them set up shop in his downtown Palo Alto office, then North Bridge Ventures gave them free rent at their office too. They were two lawyers needing to build a tech team fast to crank out code. Employee #1 was a Stanford sophomore who'd helped develop the Ravel prototype during the weekend hackathons. Two more university programmers were quickly hired. One slept on the office couch. "The North Bridge guys just loved it," said Daniel. "They thought it was the coolest thing to have this startup vibe." Daniel and Nik weren't so sure. They were rookies. Outsiders, lacking technical expertise and a strong referral network, these two non-practicing lawyers struggled to properly evaluate technical candidates. To their dismay they soon discovered that one of their newly hired Stanford programmers wasn't so hot. Daniel considered firing him, but with just five people, he fretted about losing 20 percent of his team.

The programmer stayed. Daniel and Nik were burning through their million-plus, following the faltering trajectory of a classic Silicon Valley flop – non-tech founders failing to hire a solid CTO. But the confidence they'd gained from Launchpad helped them keep moving forward. They tackled other milestones. They desperately needed content. The Library of Congress was out of reach and Stanford's law library wasn't sufficiently comprehensive. And that was precisely the point at which Daniel put on his Outsider's hat.

Daniel had taken a torts class with Jonathan Zittrain, a tech-savvy visiting Harvard professor of Internet law who happened to be the director of the prestigious university's law library. He was also a Silicon Valley insider. Zittrain stayed with Sergey Brin when he was in Palo Alto, hung with tech billionaires at Davos, and wrote prescient op-eds for the *New York Times*. Daniel reached out. Upon learning that Zittrain was going to be in town that January, he casually suggested they grab a "fro-yo" at the artisanal frozen yogurt shop on nearby Hamilton Street. This was the classic Outsider's side door. This seemingly social meeting didn't fit any predefined business objective. But Daniel didn't know any better. Between bites he told his old professor all about Ravel's technical challenges, and how they needed content. Zittrain happened to be experimenting with digitizing books and course materials at Harvard. He was considering launching a non-profit fundraising campaign to support the cause. "That's really interesting," said Daniel, jumping on the opening, "I wonder how we can help?"

That brief serendipitous encounter was the spark. Daniel and Nik immediately began brainstorming a radical, out-of-the-box idea: how they might collaborate with Harvard to digitize its world-leading legal library? As they wrote furiously at the whiteboard, one of the North Bridge investors happened to stroll in.

"Hey, what are you guys working on?"

They told him. "That's really interesting," said the investor. "I'd write a check for that." Daniel and Nik did a double take.

"Really?"

"Yeah."

Just like that, they were off and running. They fired off a multimillion-dollar proposal to Zittrain. "Hey, we might be able to do more than just help," they wrote. "What do you think about potentially partnering if we were able to fund this?"

It took time. It took a new several-million-dollar investment round in Ravel. It took lawyering. Ravel and Harvard signed a memo of understanding in November of 2013, and a final agreement in July of 2015, breaking the news that October in a major *New York Times* story that put Ravel on the map with an unlikely and stunning early content victory over other would-be startup competitors. LexisNexis and Thompson Reuters Westlaw, the two giants who dominated legal research, were put on notice. The reporter underlined the significance of Ravel's "visual" legal search innovation, trumpeted the several million dollars the company was paying to support the massive undertaking of scanning Harvard's library, and put the startup right at the forefront of a "commercial market surpassing $8 billion."

The Times article was gold. Daniel was barely thirty, a tech

184 | The Test

rookie. Yet here he was, announcing this historical agreement with Harvard, on the verge of changing how hundreds of thousands of lawyers researched cases and judges. Harvard produced a professional video starring the two co-founders. Daniel spoke of how they were working to "redefine legal research" by building tools and analytics "to empower lawyers to make data-driven decisions and sift through millions of documents to find what matters," while Zittrain underlined the scope of this huge milestone. "For the first time in history," he said, "anyone with an Internet connection will have far-ranging access to one of the largest collections of legal materials in the world."

Daniel Lewis, the Outsider, had done it, somehow outmaneuvered the world's largest legal search firms to score a golden content deal with Harvard.

Now it was down to the end game. How to scale?

The Guardian
Karoli Tells Her Story

Karoli put it out there just weeks after getting her funding: Her MVP, her minimal viable product. That's what entrepreneurs do. Prototype and iterate. See what sticks. Pivot. The Lean Startup paragon you read so much about. But in real life, entrepreneurs tend to think their MVP is pretty darn awesome, and Karoli failed to anticipate this outcome: the world couldn't care less.

Ever resilient, Karoli brushed off the setback, and hustled up an interview with the influential TechCrunch. She felt a jolt of excitement when the brief article went live, with what sounded like a plug for her marketplace for "short-term jobs with life-changing experiences." But suddenly the article took a more jaded turn. "The Jobbatical CEO tried to convince me that I had done just that [taken a Jobbatical] when I left journalism to 'do a startup', only to return a year later after I'd failed to change the world." Karoli had just flunked her first media test. The article was a clunker.

It had been hard enough to get her initial funding, but this new phase offered fresh challenges. As a Guardian, Karoli dialed in on her purpose and mission. Yet she acutely felt her fragile stature as a newly minted startup founder. And because Jobbatical required fairly complex tech engineering to catch fire, there could only be two outcomes. Live or die. Attract more funding in the next year or run out of gas.

Karoli kept pushing, flying a few weeks later to Dublin for Web Summit, Europe's biggest tech conference, pitching so many times over the next two days at her booth that she lost her voice: *Jobbatical is for short-term, international hiring… Jobbatical is for short-term international hiring…Jobbatical is for short-term international hiring.* That was her niche, her target market. There was only one problem. Her product offering was just a hazy idea, born of that flash of insight while jogging near

Singularity. She'd never tested it with real customers, and now that her MVP was live, her story was not resonating. Not at Web Summit, and not when she returned to Estonia. Employers flatly informed her that they didn't want to onboard anyone short-term, suggesting that this "limiting factor" was a blunder. Tremendous feedback, except that Karoli "wasn't that good at listening."

Good things tend to happen to dedicated entrepreneurs when they are under duress. At exactly the right time, the ideal mentor spun into Karoli's life, proving that Guardians need like-minded champions to grow and flourish. Her name was April Rinne, a trendspotting go-getter, a "global citizen" known for connecting people, ideas, and resources, and making stuff happen. Rinne had the credentials: Fulbright scholar, Harvard Law, Fletcher School at Tufts. She had traveled to over a hundred countries and worked in almost twenty nearly every year. She personified the Jobbatical concept. Governments and corporations hired Rinne to deliver inspiring keynotes and consult on the future of work, travel, and sustainable development. Rinne spotted something remarkable in Karoli and reached out. Impressed not just by her idea, but "by her hunger and grit. The way she saw the world. Her openness and her drive."

This time Karoli listened. Rinne was an ambassador from a new emerging global support system for entrepreneurs, a world of talented women and men who can't resist becoming part of something bigger, especially when aligned around a meaningful social cause. She saw herself in Karoli, and their personal bond developed into a new role as an official Jobbatical advisor. Rinne suggested Karoli try a media reboot and sent a query to a writer at *Fast Company*. Would she like an introduction to an Estonian startup "at the intersection of the future of work, talent and travel?"

The writer replied enthusiastically, promptly interviewed Karoli, and published "Need A Break From Home, But Want To Keep Working? Take A Jobbatical." The upbeat *Fast Company* story highlighted how the platform was quickly building momentum and handed Karoli a prominent soap box for her vision. "Looking at the younger generation, people value the journey over results," Karoli confidently told *Fast Company*. "I would love to have more people stepping out of their comfort zone and making their dreams happen."

The Fast Company piece provided Karoli instant traction, spawning many more articles and industry buzz, demonstrating how media can give a startup a boost. Suddenly, Karoli recalled, "really interesting people wanted to join Jobbatical." The infusion of talent helped her to start "to think more seriously about what worked and what didn't," and to question her focus on short-term hires.

It was a crazy time at Jobbatical that summer of 2015. Flooded with emails and social media notifications, Karoli could be excused for overlooking a single message, especially on Twitter. Two weeks later, she did a double take. Somehow, she'd missed a ping from Union Square Ventures, as she put it, "one of the best VCs on the planet, reaching out to talk." USV boasted a billion-dollar exit every year since 2011, with picks including Zynga, Indeed, Tumblr, Twitter, LendingClub, Etsy. *Oh my God, what have I done?* Karoli panicked at missing the lead. But she was a very good poker player. She wrote back calmly, as if she was in the habit of keeping famous VC firms on hold: "Very good," she said. "Let's have a call."

Within seconds of getting on the phone shortly thereafter, she knew all she had to do was listen. "The call was very memorable because it was a VC telling me for thirteen minutes why he thought Jobbatical would change the world." Karoli found herself not having to say a word. "Such a cool conversation. He was talking about the movement: how more people were becoming digital nomads, how mobility was transforming the way we work."

The dynamic had shifted. Karoli's cause was attracting high-level backers and believers — music to her Guardian ears. The Jobbatical story was selling itself, the money flowing. That fall, Karoli would raise another $500,000 from her angels, taking her into 2016, when Union Square Ventures would lead a $2-million round with

LocalGlobe. Karoli had come a long way from that day the all-male Estonian investor group had sent her packing. Backed by $3 million in total investment, and now featured in the portfolio of one of the world's most famous VC firms, Karoli was well positioned for the next challenge – the nut she had yet to crack, how to focus Jobbatical and find a business model that would scale.

The Visionary
Risto Goes for Big Blue

Just months after moving all the way from Helsinki to Palo Alto, Risto Lähdesmäki confronted a problem he flipped into an opportunity. He had to spend several days in Toronto to get a stamp on his documentation, a prerequisite to his formal US work permit. But Risto wasn't about to cool his heels for a week. The Visionary hustled up appointments.

Karel Vredenburg, Director of Design at IBM, happened to be in Toronto. Risto had long admired his work. "The grandfather of UI, UX design. Been at IBM for 25 years." Vredenburg had started in cognitive science and clinical psychology before specializing in design. He was a legend, who'd brought user-centered design to IBM in the early 90s and implemented design thinking at the firm a generation later. To Risto Vredenburg was The Man. He led IBM's designers. His fingerprints were on nearly every major new IBM initiative, and somehow Risto landed a meeting.

It turned out to be one hell of a test. By now, this natural showman was really, really good at showing his portfolio. He'd trimmed out all the Nokia stuff. Cued up just the right slides and images. He told his best stories, and Vredenburg was impressed. He offered a small project, and the ecstatic Finn returned to Palo Alto with high hopes, and then ran smack into corporate bureaucracy. His tiny design studio was not an approved IBM vendor. Nor was it going to be easy to become one. "He tried to get us to work on something, but we couldn't get through the procurement process."

Risto's firm was too small. Too unproven.

Nearly a year passed before Risto got a call. IBM was looking for just one or two agencies to help undertake a massive, multi-year design transformation. The kind of opportunity that would transform a small UX company. Idean was invited to compete. This time they were truly in the game. "That one single meeting in Toronto led to another meeting in Palo Alto where I met the IBM guys," said Risto. "That started a nine-month-long journey where we were part of the RFP process."

Twenty firms were invited to compete for a job that would bring international cachet and tens of millions in fees. The Visionary in Risto sensed how big this could be. The chance to initiate the pivotal design transformation of one of the world's largest tech firms. This was about far more than IBM. A once-in-a-generation economic shift was sweeping across major corporations. "Digital transformation" was all the rage. By 2018, major enterprises were expected to invest a stunning $1 trillion in digital design efforts in a single year, rushing to stay relevant, to avoid being rendered obsolete by the Amazons, Ubers, and Airbnbs of their industries. "When I heard what they were up to, that they're making probably the most significant design transformation program of all time," Risto recalled, "I was like, 'We need to be part of that!'"

The sheer size and complexity of the work was a big reason the transformation would be so momentous, a sign of how digital design could have an outsized effect on a company's business and future. IBM was the elephant, with 434,000 employees, and annual revenue just shy of $100 billion. Risto was the ant: sixteen people in Palo Alto, with another 40 or so in Helsinki.

A few months later, Risto met the key people at IBM and quickly hit it off with Phil Gilbert, IBM's General Manager of Design. Gilbert had brought an empathy-centric foundation to IBM, introducing "The Loop", a method of observing users, reflecting, and then creating. He also championed "Playbacks," open sessions in which a team shows an in-progress work to a broader set of stakeholders. Gilbert had also been an entrepreneur. He gave inspirational talks with titles like. "Every Day is a Prototype." Risto was impressed by his charisma and leadership. "I just felt like we were made for each other," he said. "I wanted to be like him."

The hard work began. "The proposal ran over 800 pages, and

took more than two months to put together. It cost Risto hundreds of thousands of dollars in lost revenue. "I've never put this much effort into anything." IBM even came to visit his Palo Alto studio, the little blue house around the corner from the iconic Apple store. The importance of winning had never hit Risto quite so hard. "I felt like we were second place so many times, and that's the worst place to be, right?"

Nine months later there was this awards ceremony. "We were sitting at the house on Kipling Street in the smallest room possible, with a lousy loudspeaker," recalled Risto. The IBM sourcing people were announcing the results. The call kept cutting in and out. Then it happened, they heard it through the bad connection. Risto, this visionary Finn – who only a couple of years before had embodied the "fake it til you make it" mantra, pretending to have an office in Palo Alto, when he truly lived in Helsinki – had won!

He'd done it by always thinking ahead. By rejecting the standard advice to play it safe, by bending the rules, by taking massive gambles. Most of all, perhaps, by being a Visionary, and always imagining what wasn't yet there – two to three years out. And now, jumping around and high-fiving his team, the seriousness of this monumental contract hit home. Risto had little time to celebrate. To win the proposal, he'd had to boldly push his own future, to promise to open a studio in Austin. IBM had not forgotten. On the call, the company had a simple request. When should they schedule the Austin studio opening ceremony?

"So, I was freaking," recalled Risto. "I needed to find talent to run the place!"

The Conductor
Carlos Goes Off-Menu

Carlos was ready to make a deal on his brand-new food truck park in San Francisco's up-and-coming Mission Bay. It was not going to be easy. "The city owned the land, they were leasing it to the agency, then leasing it to me." Carlos's lawyers had concerns about the complicated agreement. Negotiations dragged on for two months, and then finally the contract was signed.

Carlos was thrilled. With the backing of the Mission Bay Development Group and San Francisco, Carlos could hire and delegate, freeing him to truly play the Conductor. Visiting foggy Carmel south of San Francisco, he'd spent a fun Saturday night at a posh hotel with friends huddled around a gas-burning fire pit and was amazed at how that signature element brought them together. That emotional connection turned out to be quite literally the spark of inspiration for his new design.

Spark. Carlos went with the name, developed the concept, and built. He marked the park's four corners with comfortable Adirondack chairs arranged around gas-burning fire pits and outfitted with wooden sticks, chocolate bars, graham crackers and marshmallows. All the fixings for s'mores, that classic American campfire dessert. The entrance too was dramatic. Carlos dropped in a bright red English double-decker bus with an open top – a whimsical perch and colorful backdrop for bands and events. Retro wooden signs placed around the park playfully displayed distances to nearby destinations: the Spark bar, the food trucks, the fire pits, the adjacent soccer field, even iconic San Francisco destinations such as the Golden Gate Bridge. Spark was itself a ready-made tourist destination, a fresh model for food and entertainment. Carlos could already sense its potential. He'd booked ten corporate parties for several thousand guests, and the charismatic Giants outfielder Hunter Pence had chosen the park for his upcoming wedding reception. All this before Spark's summer 2016 blockbuster two-thousand-strong champagne-and-oysters gala opening.

•

The following summer Carlos was sitting among the crowd at Spark, enjoying a beer with his dad. It was a Friday happy hour, the park buzzing with a thousand people eating and drinking on a warm afternoon. "We were just like, 'Man, what did we create? This monster, amazing space.'" Father and son started talking about how Spark was bursting at the seams. They needed more space. They needed to protect their investment. They needed to think big.

"I wonder what they're doing across the street?" Carlos ventured, gesturing toward a large vacant lot. Father and son began spitballing. They couldn't set up yet another food truck park right next to Spark. Muela Senior mused: "How about something for the kids?" He paused and finished his thought, "How about mini-golf?"

Carlos thought it was a great idea. Miniature golf would appeal to families, millennials and tourists. And, perhaps even cooler: it was a fun, new challenge for the entrepreneur. Carlos knew nothing about mini-golf parks, and his plate was full with two booming food truck parks and an expanding events business. But that Monday, Carlos excitedly phoned Laura Tepper of the Mission Bay Development Group, and she too thought the idea had promise. She invited Carlos to come to the neighborhood community meeting and present to the stakeholders.

He knew many in the neighborhood had been hesitant about Spark and had only come around when his vision came to life. "Hey, I'm gonna present this idea," he recalled thinking. "If the neighborhood says no, they don't want a mini-golf course here, then I don't pursue it, right?" But the group loved the idea, voted during the meeting, and Carlos was promptly given the green light, a perfect example of selling a product before it's been designed or built. Tepper did some initial layouts and renderings, and they began hashing out a licensing agreement. Word quickly got out in the neighborhood, and poof! – like magic, Car-

194 | The Test

los got an email from Esther and Jan, a couple who by chance lived at the nearby Madrone Tower, two women crazy about mini-golf.

The stars were aligning. "They were gonna do a mini-golf course," said Carlos. "They actually had this property in Lake Tahoe with the idea of building out a mini-golf course." Esther and Jan already had a fabricator and complete plans. Carlos leaned into his pitch. How could they argue with this location, right by their new San Francisco home? Carlos had a booming business across the street. He would bring them thousands of customers.

"Why don't you just do it here?" Carlos ventured, more statement than question. On one level, it all seemed ridiculous. The tremendous coincidence, the size of his ask. For one thing, their proposed mini-golf park had a Tahoe-based theme. But Carlos kept at it. They could tweak their design for San Francisco. "I just had faith," he said. "I don't know how it happened. That's the beauty of it." The idea snowballed, and Esther and Jan said yes. He'd found his concertmasters. This was December of 2017. They hoped to have the first 18 holes open the following summer.

Carlos was discovering what happens when you boldly create the right concept at the right time, build a platform, and reap the returns of a "network effect." The Conductor soon got a call from Erika Elliott, a West Coast leasing agent for Colliers International. Elliott had the contract for leasing all the vacant storefronts in Mission Bay, storefronts that were now mostly full in part because Carlos's Spark had injected life into the new neighborhood. Erika had big news. "Hey, we've got this huge deal. The contract for the Salesforce Transbay Terminal, which is gonna be the biggest project for years and years in the Bay Area. There will be absolutely zero retail for a while." Carlos could have finished her thought. Sure enough, she recounted how her colleagues had thrown out the idea of "getting a bunch of food trucks and beer gardens and all this interim use stuff." Erika then went on to have this same food-truck-themed conversation with the folks from the Transbay Joint Powers Authority.

"I know the guy," she told them. "I know the guy to talk to."

The Leader
Allan Builds a Longer Runway

Allan Young was onto his next thing, buoyed by the success of Runway. Allan's stylish accelerator in the iconic Twitter building had become a symbol of SF's new status as the global capital of tech and entrepreneurism. Delegations and corporate groups from Europe, Latin America, China and the US visited for events and immersive programs. Allan's "accidental collisions" quickly had the designed effect. Numerous Runway startups rocketed ahead through hard work and a robust support system. He'd created a network and community focused on growth. Allan and his team introduced the companies to key partners, investors, even helping them gain crucial first sales. "We did some really concrete things to help many of our companies grow and if someone was taking a tally or doing the stats behind it, I believe that Runway was one of the most successful incubators in the world at the time. We had more companies raising more money faster."

Indeed, Runway's hot squads grew so quickly — from an initial two to three team members to a staff of eight or more — that it was time for many to fly the coop, and Allan encouraged them "to find their own place and build their own office and culture." But where? This entrepreneurial wave was so new in San Francisco, London, Europe, and Asia, that there had yet to emerge a measured approach for next steps if a startup survived the early months.

Starting up was great, but it was a far greater task to scale, and Allan had seen up close that startups had different needs. While some could only expand by attracting angel and VC investment, many other promising enterprises did not find it so easy to grab gobs of capital.

The Leader in Allan dreamed of creating another entrepreneurial hub, designed to facilitate the second, often ignored stage of a rocketing startup. Allan called this new accelerator model TopLine. The economics were similar to Runway's, but the objective radically different. TopLine was designed for eight large teams that needed to quickly expand staff and ignite sales. Allan took a long-term lease on a 40,000-square-foot building – the size of twenty homes – in the Richmond Marina across San Francisco Bay.

TopLine had none of the beautiful open architecture of Runway. No premium fixtures. No stylish furniture. "This was, 'Let's get down and dirty and get revenue,'" said Allan. "We had a sea of cubicles, and I dragged in the fattest pipes I could buy, so that every company could have their own call center and start dialing for dollars." TopLine did not look or behave like a tech incubator. Allan was adopting an entrepreneurial tech approach to a distinctly old-school method for generating revenue. He knew that many successful enterprise software startups "all have this boiler room environment, where you're just calling for revenue. You have to call and create tension for someone to buy."

TopLine went live in mid-2014. Allan had no idea what might happen. He considered it an experiment, and right off the bat, two of his eight initial tenants exceeded expectations. "They started growing so fast. One company raised 10 million dollars from Andreessen Horowitz, and two of the eight companies ended up leasing the whole space." The viral velocity of startup biology caught Allan by surprise. "That was an outcome that I hadn't anticipated, right? I didn't see that far." The San Francisco Bay Area tech ecosystem was hurtling through an explosive phase, an all-out land rush to grab space for startups and tech firms. Allan quickly made another TopLine-styled bet, taking a long-term lease on a massive building in the red hot SoMa tech district.

Allan had anticipated this second, maturing stage of startups, and jumped on this growth curve so early that he was...almost bored. Real estate struck Allan as a remarkably easy way to make money, so easy that he felt a bit guilty. Until something happened he couldn't have foreseen. Something that would test this man who'd joined the Marines simply to build character.

One day, out of the blue, Allan felt a numbness in his feet that soon spread to his fingertips. "Once it hit my lips I thought, *whoa, something's really wrong.*" He did a quick online self-diagnosis, found "a lot of scary stuff" and rushed to the emergency room. He recited his symptoms, and the intake nurse threw out a couple dark possibilities – Multiple sclerosis and ALS, Lou Gehrig's disease. Allan was terrified. "I thought I was going to die. I remember telling Cynthia, I just want them to release me for the evening so I can go home and say goodbye to the kids." Finally, a neurologist came and checked Allan's eyes, and did a number of tests, including his reflexes. It wasn't ALS or MS. Those diseases don't move that fast. Allan had contracted Guillain-Barré Syndrome (GBS), a rapid-onset muscle weakness caused by the immune system damaging the peripheral nervous system.

"There's no cure, there's no medicine for it," the doctor told Allan of the debilitating virus. "But most people recover and live normal lives." Oddly enough, at hearing the serious diagnosis, Allan felt a sense of relief. "I felt like a lucky guy." He wasn't going to die. Then he realized his sudden illness posed a different entrepreneurial challenge. He phoned his landlord, and told him about his sudden, incapacitating illness. The Andreessen Horowitz-funded startup that had taken over all 40,000 square feet of Allan's TopLine had soon outgrown the building, and now he needed to recruit new tenants. "Hey, I'm not sure I can come back and run this and find another batch of companies to build," Allan told his landlord from his hospital bed. He doubted he'd be able to do anything for a long time, let alone hustle up several startups to fill the space. "Maybe you'd be willing to release me from the lease?"

Fortunately, the landlord agreed. Allan spent three weeks in the hospital and then began the long, slow grind of rehab. His new test: learn how to walk again, to balance, to regain control of his body.

The Accidental

Mait Plays the Long Game

Mait's clutch Techstars pitch brought tens of thousands of people to the Lingvist website, people inspired by his vision, people who wanted to learn languages faster than ever before. But these same people found little of value, and quickly departed. Indeed, the limited Lingvist site exposed how sorely the erstwhile physicist needed to get up to speed as a rookie startup founder. There was only a module for English speakers to learn French, hardly a broad offering. It was, he recalled, "a miserable situation. They wanted to learn languages and they were disappointed."

Mait, a man who knew more about physics than 99.99999 percent of the world, was discovering fast that he knew next to nothing about startups. He faced a more elemental problem than their embarrassing shortage of languages. Lingvist was a technical anachronism. Their primitive MVP lived on a website, while all the popular competing products, Duolingo and Babbel, were thriving on smartphones. Nor was this easy to remedy. Lingvist had been outsourcing design, with mixed results. They needed to find a talented UX designer to develop a mobile interface, and hire a lot of other talent, and Mait was beginning to recognize that his million-plus euros would soon run out.

He improvised, turning his original Estonian-to-French version into some cash by hustling up a contract with the Estonian Ministry, Lingvist's very first paying client. Then he hunted for bigger funding. Throughout Europe there was a huge competition for EU Horizon 2020 funds. The success rate for applicants was an anemic 5 percent, but Mait desperately needed the money. He wrote a first draft, then hired an Estonian consulting firm to coach him in the specific language the government agencies were seeking. Tweaking the language worked. By late 2014, they got word that they would be granted a €1.5-million award, more than all the funding they'd received to date.

That November Lingvist's first version of its smartphone app went live at the Helsinki Slush conference. Between the hot tech conference and local news coverage in Estonia, they quickly picked up three thousand new Lingvist users. And then the Techstars tech blunder repeated itself: One step forward, two steps back. While now they had more languages and a decent smartphone interface, "the app was quite complex," said Mait. "It took 7 to 10 seconds to load, and people lost patience. People were dropping off and didn't use the mobile app." Another flop, another missed opportunity. Back to the drawing board. They needed to create a native application. A totally different design, different developers. Another setback. Said Mait: "It took months just to find the right native application developer."

Money. They needed more. Now. In April Mait fired a long shot. It had been nearly a year and a half since his CTO Tanel had met the CEO of the giant Japanese Internet firm Rakuten at Lingvist's offices in Tallinn while they were off at Slush. Mait confidently wrote the executive an email saying that he had a trip planned to Japan, and suggested they meet. This was a white lie. Mait had nothing planned at all 8,000 kilometers away in Tokyo. But it worked, and this was promising. Hiroshi Mikitani, along with heading Rakuten, was a billionaire.

Mait quickly rustled up a week of meetings in Tokyo with other major firms, such as Softbank and the Nippon Telegraph and Telephone Corporation, all strategically scheduled before his fateful meeting with Mikitani. The high-tech language-learning startup founder was accelerating his own preparation for this pivotal appointment. "I was trying to learn the Japanese business culture. I wanted to have many meetings before I met Mikitani." Mait picked up much local knowledge in those few days. It was a good thing that he could hold his liquor. "It was kind of funny, in the whole week,

I might have slept a total of 12 hours. I never got to the hotel much earlier than 5 a.m., and then had to leave at 7 for meetings." But these alcohol-fueled meetings were essential. At one, he discovered Mikitani had just published a book with his father, an economist: *The Power to Compete*. "So, I read it the night before we met. It was extremely helpful."

Mikitani had booked a meeting room for them at Rakuten in a top floor with a great view, and the two men "got along really well." When half an hour passed, Mikitani calmly asked one of his executives to take care of his next appointment. He was clearly intrigued. You don't meet a brilliant Estonian nuclear physicist every day, let alone one who has a potential solution to one of your biggest business challenges. "He was passionate about learning languages," said Mait. "He'd changed his whole Japanese corporation's working language to English to attract international talent." The two men had an animated conversation, Mikitani fascinated by the amount of technical expertise in Estonia, and how so many new products were coming together in that tiny country. Before an hour had passed, Mikitani announced that he wanted to invest.

Mait, knowing Tokyo business etiquette, had brought a present, a nice bottle of Estonian spirits signed by the most famous sumo wrestler in Japan. He'd been drinking all week. Why not? They had a toast, and then a few months later this wild shot he'd taken — pretending he had a trip planned to Tokyo, orchestrating a series of meetings so that he'd be prepared — proved to be brilliant. The startup rookie was learning the game. Rakuten led Lingvist's $8-million Series A round, bringing the total investment in Mait's startup to $11.2 million. Enough money to hire the talent.

Enough to play that long game.

The Collaborator
Joe Opens Up Shop

Silicon Valley or San Francisco?

Where to locate Capgemini's innovation hub? "One camp was hot on Palo Alto because that was where our current partners were," recalled Joe. "Cisco, Intel and the like." Then there was the advantage of being near the Sand Hill Road VCs and Stanford. But the staff who lived down in the Valley enthusiastically declared that the international city bordered by the Pacific Ocean and the Bay was where it was at: San Francisco. The hunt began. The realtors provided another compelling data point. They showed Joe and Lanny a glimpse of the future, a slick computer rendering of a seven- to ten-year projection of all the major construction projects coming online downtown, from the gigantic Salesforce tower to the massive Transbay terminal. Joe and Lanny saw that from "the perspective of talent, ecosystem and venue, San Francisco just made a lot of sense."

Their realtors took them to a lofty floor in a gleaming downtown office tower with a glorious view of the Bay Bridge, but they had their hearts set on one street in the bustling South of Market. Street level. Be part of the community, not towering above it. "There were more unicorns on Brannan than any other street on the planet," said Joe. "You've got Okta, Splunk, Dropbox, GitHub, Pinterest, Airbnb." Brannan Street was San Francisco's digital gold brick road. You could stroll twenty minutes in one direction and see how startups – and unicorns – were upending established corporations. Just down the street lay South Park, home to many of the city's VCs, perfectly situated to welcome new clients.

But finding premium ground-floor space in San Francisco's hottest neighborhood seemed almost harder than a startup trying to land its first million in investment. Capgemini had approved the budget for a modest 7,000-square-foot lease. Lanny began negotiating for a ground floor space, only to be outbid by a firm that swept in to take the entire several-floor building. Three times they lost out until finally they found a 20,000-square-foot space with a generous street-level footprint. "We started the negotiation, and then we realized the only way we could get the first floor was to take the entire building," said Joe. "Lanny made a call to our financial officer, and said, 'Hey, if I'm gonna negotiate, I gotta be able to take the whole building, and that's double the budget.'"

It was a testament to just how much Capgemini was willing to risk to get it right. Lose this space, Lanny made clear, and another might not become available for six months or more. Capgemini's CFO gave the green light on the spot, and Lanny took the whole building that spring of 2015.

•

Several months later, in January of 2016, Joe and Lanny opened Capgemini's Applied Innovation Exchange at 425 Brannan Street. The street-level entrance welcomed visitors with the casual elegance of a fashionable French café, fronting a generous event space flanked by large conference rooms with retractable doors that could be opened for spillover event seating. Clients' product innovations were showcased in impromptu exhibits throughout the space. As a Collaborator, Joe knew that bringing people together was the surest way to jumpstart creative ideas. The design was meant to enhance engagement – and action. The AIE was where the "exchange" would take place, where clients could see and act on the latest applied innovations. The world didn't need another traditional innovation showroom. "We tried to counter that trend," said Joe. "Make it about the outcome."

This was a test. "The first year we were more a visit on a trip," recalled Joe. "We had some amazing experiences where clients would be on a four- or five-day journey here. They'd go to Facebook, Google, Singularity and Stanford." Joe and Lanny learned to strategically position the Exchange as the last place senior executives would visit. This was about putting in context what they'd just seen.

The group might be ten to twenty executives or managers at a time. They'd give half of them a tour of the Exchange, while the other half settled into a room with a giant whiteboard, accompanied by a professional facilitator and storyboard artist. They'd brainstorm together with a "download" of everything they'd just experienced. Facilitators would ask them to imagine what challenges they'd face in the next six months. The next year. Three years. "You'd start to see them riffing off each other," said Joe. "They're putting it in context. They're giving us the IP that they've just gathered. And we'd do it in a way that they can see it." The artist would translate the brainstorming into images, providing a visual framework. At the end, they'd bring in the other group that had just toured the Exchange, and ask, "What would you add? What would you build? What would you take away?"

The goal was to leap out three or more years – to "Horizon Three" in the famous McKinsey model of business growth, to generate ideas for new future-leaning ventures such as research projects, partnerships, pilot programs, transformative technologies and business practices. To help clients understand fast approaching vulnerabilities and uncover outsized opportunities. In truth, Joe and Lanny were just getting started on a multi-year partnership. The Applied Innovation Exchange was a prototype. But they'd established a critical beachhead. They were developing a process and method. A collaborative, human approach to help some of the world's largest companies find the future.

This was just the first stage of what often grew into a long engagement. The objective was to balance on three time scales – short, mid and long term. To expose the client to the realities of a far larger transformation. To leap farther out, to generate ideas for new future-leaning ventures such as research projects, partnerships, pilot programs, transformative technologies and business practices. "Firms needed to navigate and engage the emerging tech landscape," said Joe. "They had to learn to listen to customers, and find fresh ways of working, and adapting their cultures."

The goal went right to the name of Capgemini's new center

on Brannan Street. "This was about applying innovation," said Joe. "To challenge the thinking of leaders." Joe was learning that for a corporate transformation to succeed, several essential human elements needed to be in place. "You can't push the tech, the business must pull," he explained. "And for the pull to be there, a purpose is needed.

So just as he had come out of his shell as a young man, and later found his voice in his first major jobs, Joe took concrete steps to change and adapt. He set out to engage with strong role models at the vanguard of an inspirational movement in leadership. Joe was seeking his own personal lighthouse, one that might show the way for others. His aim? To discover how to cultivate "a new breed of leader." The kind of man or woman who brought the critical strength and breadth to help a company evolve, innovate and transform.

He began his search by looking within.

The Athlete

Joel Troubleshoots

Joel was walking the streets of San Francisco, rolling a fashionable aluminum Pelican case and hoisting a heavy Thule bag. He was pounding the pavement, making cold calls with balance boards in toe. Would tech firms see his Level as the next must-have accoutrement? Parking his car on Potrero Street near the offices of Strava, he felt that he was in the perfect spot. The hot Strava app with its millions of enthusiastic users was all about creating tribes of athletes, and one of their tag lines, "Building the home for your active life," seemed tailor-made for his workplace innovation. Strava also happened to be flush with VC funding, and its athletic twenty-something staffers would be ideal early corporate adopters. Joel, ever the Athlete, was putting himself out there, improvising, hustling, and it seemed natural to try on the sales hat.

As Joel walked up to the Strava entrance he glanced at his phone and felt a knot tighten in his stomach: his contact at the company had canceled. Joel stopped in his tracks and considered leaving. But he went in anyway, handed the receptionist one of the three boards he'd been lugging around, and as the saying goes, when one door closes, another opens. A new email came in as he exited the lobby. Joel saw the local area code and punched in the number. A guy named Mikey answered, and said, "Yeah, we want to try it out." Joel replied that he just happened to be in San Francisco. "I'm just here today," he explained. " I have my samples in a suitcase, and I'm going through town." Joel moved to lock down the meeting: "What's your address?"

It was nearby, in San Francisco's hot SoMa tech zone. Joel didn't know what company it was yet, but after the disappointing Strava cancellation, he didn't care. This guy at least wanted a demo. Walking up to the office tower, his heart quickened. This was Google. Joel took the elevator up, and Mikey, a senior Google engineer, greeted him and invited him into an office with a killer view of San Francisco Bay. Mikey promptly hopped on the Level, and the parade began: one by one, young engineers streamed in for a spin. An astounding one hundred Googlers in a marathon four-hour stretch, during which Joel was invited to a generous lunch at the Google café. On Monday, Mikey had the Google facilities director call him, and a week later an order came in for a hundred Levels, followed quickly by a large requisition from Adidas.

Joel was rolling. He had demand, but supply was another story. Manufacturing was proving tricky. Joel wanted to assemble his boards locally, and to achieve that goal, he'd had to order the tooling to be made in China. Finally, after months of waiting, the tooling was set to arrive. Or not. His Los Angeles-based manufacturer discovered that the Chinese toolmaker had slipped and put the tooling on a later boat. Joel steeled himself for a two-week delay until late March. And then, Joel had a stroke of extraordinary bad luck: a massive, longshoremen's strike that shut down the Port of Los Angeles and jammed up 30 other ports all down the West Coast. His Chinese-made tooling was in limbo, sitting in a giant container ship just outside the port, surrounded by dozens of other container ships, going nowhere. A competitive swimmer, the Athlete in him couldn't help but think, *if only I could swim out there.*

Joel updated his Indiegogo backers on the delays. Once, twice, three times. What if he improvised and hustled? The tooling for the sandcasting prototyping process was only 300 miles away in San Francisco. It worked just fine. The mold produced high quality Levels. Why not? His Indiegogo page updates told the story in painful detail, one repeated a thousand times by entrepreneurs caught between needing to get product to early backers and eking out some modest profit. "You could see our mental anguish," Joel said, as it gradually became clear that they had "to do the right thing by the consumer." So, Joel began producing prototype sandcasted parts for the early boards, a decision that tripled his projected cost on the first 3,000 units – a $60,000 hit. "These were all the really expensive kind," he said. "Call them upgrades, call them whatever you want. All of the parts that were only supposed to go into prototype models."

Joel bit the bullet and shipped the first big batch of promised Levels to his Indiegogo backers roughly on time. But he couldn't survive if he had to produce boards that way. When the strike finally ended, Joel rushed down the coast to LA to check out the tooling, and quickly discovered a new hurdle. "The first parts came out, and they were wobbly. They were askew." The timing was horrible. FluidStance's e-commerce site was ready to go, but Joel couldn't accept online orders if he had no way to economically manufacture boards. Joel troubleshooted. He eliminated the wood deck as a probability, and considered other possibilities, including the chance that the tooling had been made in the wrong dimensions. "Did I make a mistake along the way?" he wondered. "Did the manufacturer make a mistake?" Joel huddled with his manufacturer. He'd planned to make his public launch in June at the Los Angeles Dwell on Design show. He had to solve this fast, or fail to capitalize on the demand.

How to solve it? Experiments. Research. By trial and error, Joel and his LA manufacturer discovered that because they were peeling the part off the ejector while it was still too hot, an imperfect shape was created, and thus a bit of wobbling. "Secondary processes were needed," said Joel. "We ended up spending more money on that." And Joel quickly devised a crude test to see if the new parts were up to snuff. You could call it makeshift or impromptu. There certainly might have been a more sophisticated method. But why not? "I was literally driving my truck over these parts to see if they'd fail." His logic was brutally simple. If it could hold the weight of his truck, "I'd know we were good to send this thing out. I remember thinking, *Can you break it?*" The new, improved parts passed Joel's truck test, FluidStance's e-commerce site went live, and the Level drew a big crowd at the show, and earned a nice write-up and photo in the magazine's feature article: *Dwell's 13 of the Biggest Hits from Dwell on Design Los Angeles 2015*. That June, for the first time, Joel was producing parts in LA and doing final assembly in Santa Barbara. He'd survived the trial of the longshoremen's strike and the last-minute tooling snafu. No more costly sandcasted prototypes.

He was making money on each Level he sent out to a customer. "It wasn't until Dwell that I exhaled," said Joel. "Okay, we can get this done."

The Evangelist
Uwe Makes His Big Pitch

Uwe was one to watch at the 2017 Web Summit in Lisbon. He had style: the flamboyant hair of a former concert pianist, a bright red scarf knotted around his neck, and snappy, vibrant yellow Timberland boots. Uwe had charisma, and a story to tell. Bounding onto the stage, he demonstrated with perfect pace the classic founders' talking points.

Twelve hundred startups entered Pitch at Web Summit that year, the top 200 founders pitching on three simultaneous stages for three solid days at the massive, 60,000-attendee conference. The spectacle was not unlike a marathon dance contest, demanding flair as well as stamina.

Uwe seemed to know all the right moves. He began with the pain. "A couple of years ago my brother nearly died because the hotel froze his medication by accident," he began. "So, I started doing some research and I found out something absolutely amazing. About five percent of the world's population takes medication that has to be kept in the fridge. We're talking about MS, cancer, diabetes….In fact, today out of the ten top-selling medications in the world, seven need to be kept refrigerated. So, these people are basically prisoners of their medications." The tragic result, Uwe continued, a crisis of non-adherence that harms millions and "costs $350 billion in the United States alone." Uwe had nailed the pain in twenty seconds. He'd hooked his audience. Landed the first third of the classic, three-act pitch.

Uwe pitched and pitched and pitched over the next couple days, and his story and delivery never failed to charm the judges and the audience. So what if his Kickstarter had flopped? He was back in the ring. Uwe made it all the way to the quarterfinals, then into the semis, and to the final round, where he found himself in his element, strangely relaxed before a packed basketball-stadium-sized crowd of 12,000. After all, he was the Evangelist with a powerful message to share with the world. The fact that he knew how to perform under pressure sure didn't hurt.

On stage, the entrepreneur calmly closed in on The Solution: "LifeinaBox is the world's smallest fridge. You can put up to one month's worth of medication inside. Why connect the fridge to an application? It will monitor the temperature of the medication. It will monitor the battery. It will also set your reminders. Today I have a 12-hour battery. It plugs into any power source…We designed the product so that it can be assembled like a Lego system…by hand-icapped people in France…We have huge ambitions. An incredible team. Doctors. Scientists. We've already started the next genera-tion," he said, motioning to a pen-sized model displayed on the giant screen behind him. "This is LifeinaTube. It will be available at the end of next year. The world's smallest fridge just got smaller, with LifeinaPocket."

Uwe was ready to close. With emotion: "Ladies and gentlemen, LifeinaBox is not just a fridge. LifeinaBox is a tool for the heart. It is freedom. Freedom for people to travel. Knowing that their med-ication is at exactly the right temperature, anytime, anyplace. Thank you very much!"

The crowd responded with thunderous applause to what had just been a master class in pitching. Now it was time to wait for the judges. Backstage with the three other finalists, Uwe was still skep-tical. Having won his share of contests, Uwe saw it as just another chance to take home another hunk of plastic, another trophy. But this was a bigger platform. Al Gore was also backstage, awaiting his turn as the final act after the prizes were awarded. Uwe had always admired Gore, so he went right up and told the former vice pres-ident that he loved his films, and thought he was wonderful. They shook hands, and Gore wished him good luck.

Uwe figured his odds were good. He'd always designed his slides for how people grasp new ideas visually, and hated it when people crowded their slides with text, because he knew that audiences can't help but try to read those words, at which point they stop listening. The other two finalists, well, their slides had too many words. Waiting backstage, it dawned on Uwe that this might be a big deal. As he glanced at the TV monitors, it began to sink in that his audience wasn't just the 12,000 packed into the amphitheater, but a good chunk of the 60,000 attendees, all the people outside the arena "watching these massive screens, like in Central Park." Uwe too was watching the screen. The head of the jury was at the microphone, announcing that Lifeina had taken a whopping 72 percent of the popular vote. She smiled, and said the judges agreed, "The winner is Lifeina!"

Giddy with his win, Uwe effusively congratulated the two other finalists backstage, until they told him that everyone was waiting for *him*. So this middle-aged man with the blazing red scarf and oversized yellow boots reclaimed the stage, delivered "the standard platitudes" and then promptly turned to walk off. "Hang on! Hang on!" called out the conference host. There was a moment of shock, a fresh rush of excitement, as she handed him a giant cardboard check. Uwe took in the number. He hadn't even known there was prize money, but he'd just won €50,000.

Before Uwe could let the victory sink in, they dragged him to a press conference to opine on the future of medicine. His phone was blowing up with texts and calls he couldn't possibly begin to answer. Finally, it was time to go back to the hotel. "Everybody on the street was congratulating me because I had my check under my arm," recalled Uwe. It was more than a little comical, this beaming, brightly dressed man carrying a giant check through the streets. "What are you supposed to do with a check?" a bemused Uwe recalled, "You can't leave it behind!"

The next morning, he had to go to the airport, and he still had "this stupid check! It wouldn't fit in my suitcase." So, Uwe Diegel, still wearing his signature red scarf and yellow boots, was back on the Lisbon metro, being showered with more congratulations. "And you know, I arrived at the airport, and the security guy said, 'I saw you on TV last night! I voted for you!' He waved me through, with my check and everything."

Uwe Diegel took his seat on the flight home to Paris. The Evangelist had done what he did so well, captured people's hearts and minds with a story, a cause, and yes, a product. Uwe had passed his test with flying colors. Rebounded from his Kickstarter fiasco. Beaten more than a thousand other startups, most with founders young enough to be his sons or daughters. And he had the proof, tucked conspicuously right in front of his knees, a giant €50,000 check.

Takeaways:
Passing the Test

Test. The penultimate stage that encapsulates the entrepreneur's journey. Commitment and tenacity are key. You methodically remove risks to clear the runway for the acceleration stage. Here's where you steel your resolve and strengths and begin to make leaps you didn't think possible. Who will get you through the Test?

Makers "fail faster to succeed sooner."
Outsiders launch outside the box.
Guardians sharpen their story through adversity.
Conductors experiment with new arrangements.
Leaders keep pushing boundaries.
Accidentals take long shots because they ignore the odds.
Collaborators source talent to jumpstart projects.
Athletes troubleshoot in clutch moments.
Evangelists rise to challenges under pressure.
Visionaries think ahead.

7 — The Scale —

What's next? Joe Boggio wondered. What does success look like after success?

Scale is the entrepreneur's Holy Grail, the stage when results can rocket. The crucial, earlier steps in the Arc have prepared you now to channel your vision and ambition into ever bolder actions. Scale is where you discover the size of your dreams, where sales, revenues, user base and productivity can expand beyond anything you imagined.

Yet scale can be elusive. Only a fraction of startups prove out their business model and take off. Yet we live in an era when the technology and methods available to rapidly expand sales or roll out a hit platform have never been greater. Our ten entrepreneurs have been working diligently to disrupt and remake industries but that's often not enough. Not everyone will win, a reality that venture capitalists understand all too well. Today they scour the world for startup investments and consider it a success if out of every ten firms in their portfolios, six or seven fail, a couple survive and one or two hit it big. Scale is where our characters find out where they land on this harsh metric.

Our entrepreneurs started on this journey from Estonia, Finland, South Africa, Michigan, Colorado, and California. They brought varied backgrounds and educations. Their companies and products couldn't be more different, and because of this range and authenticity their stories have brought us to the point of something rare – a virtual snapshot of what happens to ten wildly ambitious individuals willing to do what it takes to scale. The mindset of each distinct Face once again informs this, our final stage. Our Athlete, so accustomed to tackling everything on his own, takes a step back and considers how best to apply his passion and genius. The Guardian, stubbornly dedicated to her cause, faces a devilish choice. Stay the course or dare to switch tracks to what might be a faster growth path. The Evangelist flies to China to source the ideal manufacturer, the one he hopes will deliver the financial success he needs to fund his next passion project. Our Visionary, having achieved tremendous scale, has a fresh insight that just might be the next big thing.

Sometimes during The Scale, even the most locked-in entrepreneur approaches this pinnacle and faces possibilities – or obstacles – he couldn't possibly anticipate. For our Collaborator, tasked with inspiring and guiding executive teams, Scale is the point at which he looks within and ponders what success might look like after success. The Conductor has no such luck. Two turns of fate give him the greatest test of his life.

Scale is more than money. It's about satisfaction. Finding meaning and purpose. It's about your own personal growth, and deciding what you really truly want. And perhaps, what's next.

The Maker

Perry Bakes a Hundred Cakes

On a warm June day in 2019 at Terún, an Italian restaurant in downtown Palo Alto, Perry Klebahn stood before the latest cohort of eager young Stanford entrepreneurs. The ceremonial lunch marked not only the end of class but a milestone for Perry. This was Launchpad 10. The former mechanical engineering student who had studied under IDEO legends David Kelley and Dennis Boyle had been making Makers for more than a decade.

Perry's legacy was not just the half-billion-plus in capital raised by student startups under his tutelage, the more than 50 thriving companies he helped launch, or the thousands of jobs created. Along the way the Maker had picked up some formidable new skills. When Michael Dearing moved on after a few years, Perry fully embraced his Collaborator tendencies to find a new able partner in Jeremy Utley, a former consultant and graduate of Stanford's business school. Together they led Launchpad and became co-directors of Stanford d.school's Executive Education program, building it up into a robust series of design thinking bootcamps and a range of design- and customer-focused workshops for executives throughout the year. Increasingly, Perry and Jeremy take their action-oriented labs global – in the past year the duo has led engagements in Russia, Hong Kong, Australia, Malaysia and Israel.

Launchpad was an experience and, not surprisingly, on this summer day, Perry and Jeremy provided the thirty or so students a unique mixture of real-life lessons from three talented alumni. The first guest speaker highlighted just how large a role Launchpad had played in supporting entrepreneurs. Jon Beekman, the CEO of Man Crates, a startup that never garnered the early funding of that year's Daniel Lewis, but had beaten the odds to rocket to an astounding $24 million in annual sales in just a few years. Beekman knew that

Stanford and Launchpad had steeped him in a model that instilled the value of selling before you make it. "You can sell almost any concept or any idea before you really do the work to make it real," he told the students. "If today you could go out with a Square card reader, and someone says they would buy your product, whip that thing out and take their credit card."

But not every startup in Launchpad makes it big, explained Utley, as he introduced the day's second speaker, who after two years running her startup, decided to move on. "That's a reality for some of you," explained Utley. "And that's not a failure, and not a bad thing." Liz Grace, founder of Grace Portraits, a service for ordering hand-drawn custom portraits, told the class flat-out what she would have done differently: "I would have connected more. Even though this was going really well, I was one foot in, one foot out. I raised $100,000 from a friends-and-family round and that's it.... I would've hired, I would have raised more money, done more marketing." Interestingly, she confided that she'd recently learned more about archetypes, and "what motivated me as a human when I started the business." What did she know now that she wished she'd known then? "I need to have someone to bounce ideas off. So I would've been a lot more aggressive about getting a co-founder."

The final speaker that day – a driven Athlete – had thrived in Launchpad. Annie Stancliffe, sole founder of mobile nail salon High Five, capped the event with an apt metaphor for startups and Launchpad itself. Maybe creating and, more importantly, scaling a startup is like baking a great cake, she proposed. "The first year is about figuring out this recipe for your gooey carrot cake," she began. "How sweet should it be? What time of the day do they get to eat it? When do they get to buy it again?" That, she explained, was the crucial first step, getting to a "90 percent good recipe, running experiments" to find out who wants to eat your cake. "Then, you're baking a perfect carrot cake every week. You keep your ear to the ground. You're experimenting, figuring out what to tweak."

Suddenly it's all about scale. "How to bake a hundred cakes a day.

That's an entirely different set of challenges that requires different people. That's when I made my first hire and found my operations lead. Now it's where should we be? How many ovens do we need? How can we hire some bakers? And it's scary, because the stakes are higher. Well, guess what? You're going to have to make some bad cakes. It's not going to be precious anymore."

Perry was proud of these graduates and proud of what he, Michael Dearing and Jeremy Utley had achieved in this decade of Launchpad: the strong point of view they took toward doing and action, the furious pace, the decision to isolate and go deep on so many distinct elements of starting a company. And of course the inveterate Maker was preparing some tweaks for Launchpad 11. Pushing the students to become more comfortable using tools to move faster, such as requiring them to spend $200 on Upwork.com hiring freelance researchers to analyze the competition. "It scales you," explained Perry. "Meaning you need to be pitching investors and understanding your competitive landscape. You don't need to spend four hours on Google looking at all the [potential] companies."

And Perry and Jeremy were working hard to scale themselves and elevate their life's work. "If we want to make Launchpad world-class there's plenty of things we need to stop doing," said Perry. "If things are low yield and taking a lot of time, let's eliminate them. It's an editing process, so I can do the things that allow me to scale myself and make a bigger contribution."

The Maker has a hunch they will find an edge in becoming more exacting in prototyping and analytics. "We're going to do much more work around experimentation and really teach students, 'When do I need to deploy parallel prototypes? How many variables do I need to get meaningful data?'"

Achieving what Perry calls "experiment hygiene" won't be easy. He confesses he's not yet sure how to teach it successfully, but Perry and Jeremy have already begun running practice modules. In the push and shove of the intense ten weeks of Launchpad, "We want to get to a point where we can run an experiment with a prototype that has six potential variables, but we only play with one at a time."

Perry paused, excited at the prospect: "That'd be an awesome experiment."

The Evangelist
Uwe Aims for the Heart

There comes a time for an entrepreneur when it's all about economies of scale. Fresh from winning Web Summit Uwe and his wife Lily set out to do just that, to source the ideal partner to manufacture LifeinaBox in volume to make it a whopping success and fund their next dream.

They began by Googling thirty Chinese manufacturers, winnowing the list to three before hopping on a jet plane. Candidate number one: Haier, one of the world's largest manufacturers of refrigerators and home appliances, an industrial powerhouse near Beijing. The company sent a limousine to meet the couple at the airport and the next morning took them to Haier University, a pristine, high-tech 12,000-square-foot corporate training center designed to impress. Uwe was wowed. Not just by the professionalism and superior branding. "Haier is a great company. If there's a quality problem it's an occasion to make things better." The respect was mutual. Haier was eager to partner with the innovator to get into the red hot business of healthcare. The meeting began strongly, with Haier, famous for its refrigerators, making clear they loved his portable fridge for keeping medicines cool. The good vibes evolved into the open collaborative give-and-take design process Uwe loved. "We spent the whole day talking with a team of six engineers about how to make things better, and we came up with the idea of putting the batteries in the lid to give us more space." He couldn't believe this was his first meeting in China. "It was so epic and so positive!"

Next they visited a low-cost manufacturer near Shanghai they'd previously worked with, "a filthy factory with mounds of electronic components lying in the corner covered with dust." Nothing impressive here, but the scrappy owner wanted the business, and Uwe considered it a worthwhile visit because along the way he worked out that his components, including tooling, should cost about $28. Add in roughly 20 percent for assembly, 20 percent profit and he figured the minimum production cost of LifeinaBox would be approximately $40 per unit.

The third company was a world leader in thermoelectrics. Much like Haier, the CEO rolled out the red carpet. With a dramatic press of his thumbprint on a biometric lock, he opened vacuum-sealed doors to his private research lab, proudly showing them "dozens and dozens of prototypes, the technology of the future." The critical meeting with the engineers began well: "We did the presentation, and they loved the product," recalled Uwe. Except he wasn't feeling the love. "Every time I would make a suggestion, they would say, 'Oh no, this is a better way.' They were not listening. And I found it insufferable."

After returning to Paris Uwe contracted with all three manufacturers to make samples to gain a sense of both interest and capabilities. Haier seemed the clear favorite, but he wondered. Was his business "big enough" to interest them? Surprisingly, the third firm was slow to deliver a sample. Uwe counted them out: "They just weren't reactive enough."

Haier came in at four times the cost of the components – a whopping $117 – far beyond what Uwe could afford with his planned retail price point of around $230. The second firm's price was an equally shocking $28. *This is why you need to go to China*, Uwe thought. The range in quality and price was extreme – a four-fold difference. Though tempted by the profit potential with the low-end firm, Uwe knew there could be advantages in working with Haier. "They would be investing in our company, just like when they bought General Electric's appliances division. And they wanted to represent us in China, which means an investment of Haier into LifeinaBox."

Uwe knew that the more attention he could focus on himself and LifeinaBox, the stronger his bargaining position. He set out to increase his public profile, entering a few critical contests. In December of 2018, LifeinaBox won the prestigious Prix Galien award in the Connected Objects category. "The French Galien award is the equivalent of the Nobel prize for pharmaceuticals," said Uwe. "That's a kick-ass award in terms of marketing." The entrepreneur followed that up with a win in the Tech for a Better World category at the January 2019 Consumer Electronics Show in Las Vegas.

Negotiations with Haier continued, and Uwe succeeded in cutting their pricing and cementing a deal. Mass production began in May of 2019 and by that summer Uwe had shipped the first 42,000 units of LifeinaBox. It was too early to predict how big it would go, but he was heartened that the elegant device, Apple-like in its attention to small details, had virtually no returns. Meanwhile, Uwe was already onto a new passion project. A venture with BASF to develop a semi-rigid insulating foam for LifeinaBag, a protective pouch with a reusable gel pack that could insulate medications for 12 hours. He'd iterated the fridge to a pocket.

It was all practice for the bigger dream, an insulated container for transporting organs, code-named LifeinaHeart. "Today, out of a hundred hearts that are donated, seventy-three percent of them are thrown away because you have just four hours to make sure the heart arrives in the right condition," said Uwe, pausing for emphasis. "I mean, that's just criminal." Uwe had already expanded that time to six hours. He thought he could triple that life-saving window to 12 hours. "If we managed to do that, we could completely eliminate the shortage of hearts in the entire world," effused Uwe. "Come on! That's a good reason to wake up in the morning!"

Uwe was talking about investing two to three years of research, spending six hundred thousand euros of his own money, extra cash he hoped to earn with LifeinaBox and pour into this latest crusade, a mission that "you can't put a price on."

But if the Evangelist is right, he just might one day keep hundreds more hearts beating each year.

The Leader
Allan Digs for Ideas

Allan's days were dedicated to physical therapy, relearning to walk, use his hands, and speak. Six arduous months of slowly regaining his old self. With several entrepreneurial ventures and savvy investments behind him, he could now pick and choose. Hunt, as he put it. Allan had heard so many VCs parrot the boasts of giant funds that they only invest in companies introduced to them by trusted friends. The way Allan saw it, that may work for the premier US venture funds, but the rest us "have to generate and chase ideas. You have to be the truffle pig, and try to find something great. Have a view of where things are going, rather than, 'Oh, this smart guy brought me this deal, so it's interesting.'"

So Allan Young, entrepreneur and eager truffle pig, dug for ideas. Runway excelled at nourishing startups, while TopLine specialized in helping them scale. His new hunch, the third phase of the rocket's trajectory: "Let's build headquarters for unicorns. That was the thesis." He took a lease with a partner on a vast three-story self-storage building at 144 Townsend in SF's SoMa district and began remodeling, and soon the unicorn Docker swooped in to snap up the whole space. Next, one of China's biggest real estate firms entered into negotiations to buy Runway.

When you're a truffle pig, investment ideas can come from anywhere. Years before, Allan had met a man who had developed interesting technology for the legal discovery process. "We just kept talking," said Allan. "He had been studying what could be applied to AI." A few years later Allan was the first investor in this new technology to organize legal workflows. "With his domain knowledge, he started selling, and got some headlines with his customers' names – one of the largest ridesharing companies and one of the largest video game publishers." Allan invested $300,000 and a few years later the company was sold for around ten million. The sort of modest success that Allan loved in part because it didn't come served on a silver platter.

Not every hunch panned out. Allan invested in an AgTech startup with a blockchain layer that got sideswiped by the crypto crash. Yet even that failure had an upside. They'd reached out to California growers, and one of the places these growers orbited was the biotech accelerator IndieBio. There he met an intriguing biologist from New Mexico Tech, an unlikely looking businesswoman covered head to toe in tattoos. Her specialty? Cannabis. Siv Watkins and her team started 11BIOMICS to develop technology to isolate beneficial microbes from cannabis biomes, and return them to the plants at therapeutic levels. The goal: eliminating diseases such as powdery mildew. In the summer of 2019 they made a splash at IndieBio Demo Day, Allan on hand to stoke the sales funnel and talk to potential investors.

Today, Allan leads his projects on his own terms. When his mother fell ill with tuberculosis, he reduced his business commitments and drove her to her daily treatments and acupuncture appointments, and felt "lucky " to be able to do that. This too was leadership. Family leadership. "In Chinese culture, as the oldest son, you take care of your parents," he explained. "She needed me to be there to help translate from Cantonese." Allan also spends as much time as possible with his two young children, bringing them to meetings, and home schooling them with his wife. He is refreshingly real. Compared with the noxious behavior of so many tech leaders, he brings a magnanimous counter point.

Yes, he's a former high school truant. But more importantly, Allan is a self-made entrepreneur and investor, who sought out that random speaker in a hotel ballroom to find discipline, leadership, and meaning. Today, he's internalized — and externalized — those lessons to inspire those around him through his simple, authentic actions.

The Outsider

Daniel Begins "The Process"

Daniel and Nik had mastered The Money. Secured that million-plus angel round barely out of Stanford. Locked down an astonishing $8.1-million Series A round in February of 2014 to fund the digital conversion of Harvard's vast legal library and win widespread market cred. Over and over they'd proven that they could raise the heady sums needed to support a highly tech-driven startup. Daniel was clear about his objectives. "Each time we raised money it was with a set of goals in mind. Is this the pathway we want to be on? Eighteen months from now, where exactly do we want to be? What will we have accomplished? Not just for our investors. Not just to be able to raise more money, but to advance the business in ways we think are meaningful."

By 2016 they were shifting to a more mature phase. It was time to sell their software to major law firms. They had their eyes on the big prize – the chance to disrupt the established players, the multibillion-dollar powerhouses of LexisNexis and Westlaw. Yet Ravel wasn't a consumer app. It wouldn't quickly go viral. "LexisNexis sells a hundred different things. It's a big bag their salespeople carry around," said Daniel. "It became apparent to us that we were going to have to get a foot in the door and build a position in a law firm over the long term." That year they raised another round of $6 million, bringing their total funding to $15 million. A tech firm approached them about a possible acquisition. Daniel and Nik were interested, but their board and investors weren't so sure. They pushed them to just "build the business and do another fund raise in the future." The two co-founders felt they should have an option, so that summer of 2016 they took the initiative to reach out to LexisNexis. Daniel told the firm he knew they'd acquired a startup called Lex Machina, similar to

Ravel, and heard that the acquisition had gone well for both parties. "It seems like you're headed in a direction that's aligned with where we want to go," Daniel began. "Would you be interested in having a conversation?"

So began what Daniel called "the process." A handful of companies were interested, but Daniel and Nik kept coming back to LexisNexis. It took about the same time it takes to make a baby, about nine months. The multimillion-dollar price was not made public in a *Wall Street Journal* story titled "LexisNexis Snaps Up Legal Tech Startup Ravel Law." LexisNexis called it part of a broader vision "to create the data-driven lawyer of the future." Just five years after he'd attended Stanford Launchpad and earned his law degree, Daniel was still CEO of Ravel, but also now a general manager at LexisNexis. In the next two years they would release a flurry of new products, rebranding Ravel as Context, giving lawyers "insights on the precedents and language" that have been most persuasive to judges, detailed statistics and analysis on which cases they cite, and the relative success of certain motions. And they would plumb LexisNexis data on 380,000 expert witnesses to provide an expert witness scorecard.

Along the way Daniel took some time to do something completely new, to be a visiting professor in the Master in Legal Tech program at Madrid's renowned IE university. But he wasn't done with startups, and the Outsider in him was already thinking about launching something "non-law-related." There was, he said, an addictive quality to the startup journey. "The learning, autonomy, responsibility, the problem solving," he said, barely pausing to breathe, "the wearing of multiple hats, the speed, the customer feedback."

Daniel may just be getting started.

The Accidental

Mait Stumbles Onto A Wizard

Nearly eight years into Mait's accidental experiment in startup land, Lingvist, his artificial intelligence language learning firm, remained a long shot. Judged by the traditional benchmark of VC dollars and eyeballs the Estonian startup lacked the investment, advertising and marketing panache of competitors. By early 2020 competitors Duolingo and Babbel had raised $138 million and $33 million respectively, while Lingvist could only claim $11 million. Duolingo was far and away the world's most popular language learning app, with over 200 million users. Lingvist, in contrast, had just a paltry 1.4 million, ironically almost exactly the population of Mait's native, tiny Estonia.

But the game wasn't over just yet.

Mait and team began a small research project. They were a learning company, after all, so his programmers developed a modest internal tool to manually build language courses. The tool morphed. Evolved like a living thing. Then the big idea emerged, one intrinsic to a company built on machine learning and AI. Recalled Mait: "Can we make it automatic?" Soon they were doing just that, creating entire courses on the fly. Mait had language experts validate the results. "It was very exciting. It emerged organically from the team doing their work," recalled Mait. "Everybody fell in love with this piece of software."

That was nearly two years ago. Since that early prototype Mait moved to productize the concept. If Lingvist's first aim was to dramatically accelerate learning a language, this new tool provided a multiplicative effect. Languages are deep and broad, like an ocean — English has 170,000 words — and we often wish to take a targeted trip. Lingvist could now add navigation to your journey of discovery. "It starts with users adding in words or a piece of text to the platform, the app's algorithm quickly creating an entire course stemming from their input, presenting example sentences to study and stitching a huge vocabulary set together," *Language* magazine wrote in an article describing the new capabilities. "An American expat living in France who is into jazz can learn to speak about jazz in French without going through a whole language course."

Lingvist's Course Wizard launched in the summer of 2019, allowing language learners to quickly master specialized vocabulary from numerous prepared courses, say for a trip, business or even love. The learning engine speedily spun out a vast new library of specialized content. "People can really easily make their own courses. There are already more than 10,000 separate courses in four or five languages," said Mait, who believes this added personalization will be revolutionary. "We measure how people's memory works. We recall words when it's most efficient to do so. And if something is very customized you will learn faster. The magic is that the engine makes it scalable." Mait's goal is to keep scaling, to leap beyond language to the even broader massive $40 billion plus industry of EdTech. "In the next couple of years we will keep doing experiments," he promised. "As we make the unit economics work we will have more resources, more users, more data."

It's not merely about scaling through machine learning. Mait had been trying hard to elevate his own skills as a manager and leader, something he once knew precious little about as an Accidental. Working to empower an international team with staff in London, Germany, Poland, and Portugal, Mait has recently become fascinated by the work of the famous neuroscientist, Antonio Damasio, on how critical our feelings are to our thinking. "Emotions play a very important role in decisions," said the former physicist. "You've got to take care of the emotions. It's that simple. If you do, many things are far easier."

Mait has overcome so many obstacles on this curious entrepreneurial journey that began by chance seven years ago when he decided he just had to speak French. He has a long road ahead, and freely acknowledges that to go fast, he must be patient. "We don't have the same viral components of some of our competitors. Others have advertising. But we are starting to monetize our user base and are close to being cash positive."

And the startup founder targeting the burgeoning global knowledge economy may have an unexpected edge: Mait Müntel, the Accidental entrepreneur, just happens to be crazy about learning.

The Athlete

Joel Waters his Creative Side

Joel Heath built things and experiences founded in his belief in the importance of movement and flow. He'd rebelled against the tyranny of the traditional work chair to create the Level, his elegant standing board for the office. Joel was proud. He'd raised half a million dollars in his Indiegogo campaign and won the Mayo Clinic's endorsement, and yet he was keenly aware he'd chosen a tough road.

As FluidStance grew, Joel left the garage and moved into a generous office above the thriving new Impact Hub in Santa Barbara's hip Funk Zone. It was more space than he needed, but Joel was planning to expand, and quickly subleased the bulk of it to three other startups. "My thought was, I'll grow, and we can have people move out," he recalled. "But, then the wild part was, the impact of seeing these other startups grow." FluidStance was the only business with a physical product. Joel was struck by the stark differences in their experiences. "I was watching how simple updates were being made to software, while I was trying to figure out how to tweak tooling and things like that."

This was an open office, the companies under nondisclosure agreements with one another so they could work freely. Two were software firms, another in the natural foods business. "You're just hearing each other's successes and tribulations, watching management styles," he recalled. Sharing the space with other founders allowed him to "live" their experiences to gain insights for his own tactics and management. At times, he envied their ease of scaling up. "Man, did I choose a hard space," he sighed. "As my buddy says, if I had put this many resources and time into something in the natural food space, I could have retired by now."

By late August 2018 he faced a hard truth, the realization that, "I was probably preventing the business from doing what it needed to do." The Athlete was juggling too many balls on his own. He'd begun reading Leonardo Lospennato's *The Da Vinci Curse* and felt it summed up his dilemma. "I'm HR, the Janitor, the Innovator, R&D – I'm doing accounting, all this other stuff. It's dangerous, because I don't dive into my genius, if you will." And so Joel brought in a new General Manager to be the implementer, and free him to do what he did best. Create.

Obsessed with heightening human potential, the Athlete looked for another pain, and then stumbled upon a startling fact that made him think there might be a product need. He learned that even minimal dehydration negatively impacts cognitive performance, and that 75 percent of people are dehydrated at work. Next, he found the bottleneck: "Workers' hydration was dictated by their bottles' capacity versus their own." So he set out to increase their potential. To eliminate breaks in hydration, by designing the world's first "personal water tower."

Auto racing, outdoor gear, and traditional water bottles inspired his first creative brief. The initial prototype "looked part UFO, part egg," joked Heath but the design soon gelled into an elegant minimal tower with BPA free, eco-friendly materials. He turned to Indiegogo and attracted nearly the double the funding he wanted. Models began shipping in early 2020, a strong addition to his suite of healthy products for the modern office. "Hydration is a spontaneous activity," read the product description. "If water is at your fingertips, you drink."

On a roll, Joel read a story that every year we churn through 50 billion Post-its. He saw the "room between the keyboard and monitor as dead space and thought the two ideas would collide well." Design was inspired by "what we could get done locally." Joel prototyped with a nearby metal shop, and in February started shipping the Slope (inspired by ski runs), a curved personal desktop steel whiteboard to slide out over a keyboard and "lay down your thoughts while you help protect our forests." Perhaps while you're balancing on a Level. Buy one and Joel will plant a tree too.

The Visionary

The Last Pretty Girl on the Dance Floor

Risto had the vision, grit and talent to win the IBM deal. He'd opened an office in Austin, Texas, and the contracts were coming in easily. Business was accelerating, until he tripped over an old mistake. Risto had naively given veto control over critical company matters to his early Finnish investors. Now, to hire the best, Risto had to offer equity, and these stubborn Finns wouldn't give it to new hires.

That summer Risto spent a working holiday in Finland with his wife and children, a vacation spoiled by the investor war. "I spent the whole month fighting with these dudes," he recalled. "I mean they were looking for millions and millions for the value they provided, which was basically zero." Finally, Risto found some new, more reasonable Finnish investors to front the cash and pay them off. "We got rid of them, let's say, with blood," he said. "But bringing in the [new] investors at that point gave us a little bit of freedom."

Risto could now offer equity. Hire faster and expand. Suddenly, his larger vision was becoming true. "The big companies became aware that user-centered design is key to winning future clients," he recalled. "They were starting to realize that this isn't just any old thing, like you are designing furniture or things. UX design is where tech is going." The world's largest global consultancies – Accenture, Deloitte, KPMG, McKinsey and PricewaterhouseCoopers – snapped up UX firms and PR agencies right and left.

Risto was approached by bankers about acquisitions. He took meetings, but wasn't ready. Idean was right in the middle of IBM's massive design transformation project. Risto wanted to update his management and make sure potential buyers fully valued his firm. His advisor George Kadifa, a deeply experienced tech executive and investor, coached him on how to create a new framework to manage and lead Idean. The traditional core metrics of a large market, robust growth and profitability weren't enough. Risto had to prove that Idean could create "unique, protected tech" and demonstrate the potential for scale. All while giving the sense that he was one of the few UX firms left that could deliver this sorely needed capability.

The strategy and hard work paid off. Two years passed, two years in which Risto said no a few times, even to one of the world's biggest accounting firms, because he knew a structured firm like that would choke Idean's culture. Then, in the summer of 2016, a highly respected European global consultancy came calling.

Risto was sitting with his management team in Palo Alto. "Now it's going to happen," he told them. "It's going to happen." When you've spent seventeen years on something, and moved your company from Finland to California, you know a little. And Risto knew Idean had two distinct potential paths. Grow organically at a reasonable pace. Or try to leapfrog ten years ahead and transform into a major international player.

This opportunity wouldn't last forever. Risto had a saying: "I want to be the last pretty girl on the dance floor." But the music had been playing a long time and it was getting late. The first meeting with the major European consulting firm took place in New York. "I met a couple of French guys. It felt like a good date," he said. "Let's have another one." From Day One he'd hoped this would happen. "One European company with another. I felt I could work with these people."

Waiting had been wise. Risto was telling a confident, compelling story, and in the intervening years Idean's projected price to sales multiple had risen to a level rarely seen for a UX design firm. "I want to be like Pixar for Disney," he said, and Capgemini, eager to transform itself, liked the analogy. Still, Risto had plenty of worries. If the talks progressed, he would eventually have to break the news to his team. There were other suitors in the wings, and he needed to be certain this major shift would be good for his company. He loved Idean's culture and knew that even in the best of circumstances these deals are risky. And there was something else. "I was doing something I couldn't tell anyone. I couldn't even tell my wife," Risto said. "I was in a black hole for months, thinking this could be really nice if it works out … but if it doesn't happen, I'm dead."

The Collaborator
Joe Looks Within

*W*hat's next? Joe Boggio wondered. What does success look like after success?

Joe's job at Capgemini's Applied Innovation Exchange was to help visiting executives map out digital paths to unlock the future. But Joe began to see more and more that the biggest challenge was human, and so just as decades ago he had confronted his shyness by starting a Toastmasters group, he set out on a personal mission to explore a radically different kind of knowhow that would serve both his own interests and those of his clients.

Joe began researching elite, high-performing teams, and as the son of an armed service member he found himself drawn to Mark Divine, a former Navy Seal "who infused a lot of East and West thinking" through a study of Zen, yoga, and "a military-styled high-performance mindset." Joe enrolled in Divine's leadership program for a year, studying the often overlooked roles of intuition, emotion and spirit. He saw a foot doctor, had his stride analyzed, and began running. Joe lost ten pounds and ran his first marathon. Something was happening. "I cannot give words to this," he told an executive coach at the time. "But there is something in me that wants out.'"

Joe began to understand that "how you lead and operate is a function of your belief systems and unconscious biases." He started to see every moment as an opportunity for growth, repeating the oft-quoted phrase attributed to Martha Beck: *How you do anything is how you do everything.* His first executive coach helped him to see how many men and women had invested so heavily in him over the years – from that no-holds-barred Michigan trade school instructor, to a litany of professional mentors and friends. Yet now, he'd reached the point where "the next person influencing me and lighting me up is me." Joe read voraciously, including the book *Scaling Leadership*. He underwent a rigorous 360 review process to understand his "strengths, weaknesses and development areas" as an executive manager.

Joe saw even more clearly that "the element that seldom scales is leadership." He had his work cut out. He could be reactive, responding to pressures, rather than "being authored by self, where I know the outcome I want, and I welcome the resistance – because I've got confidence and capability – and I invite it." Yet he could spot a possible solution to this challenge of scaling leadership. "Once you shift your mindset and start diving into emotional intelligence and spiritual growth, you realize, *Wow, I'm at the first of a very small foothill and I can see Mount Everest now!*"

•

Joe Boggio's personal transformation happened to intersect with another one of our characters, Risto Lähdesmäki of Idean. The self-described "last pretty girl on the dance floor," said yes to his French suitors in 2017. Capgemini was dramatically expanding its own capabilities, making major acquisitions in innovation, and acquiring the hot UX design firm fit right in its plans. Risto's path as a bold Visionary now met in San Francisco with Joe's. Part of Risto's team began working in Capgemini's San Francisco office, the very same hub Joe had played such a pivotal role in creating. To Joe, Risto's presence was symbolic, a change both visual and visceral. During the first ribbon cutting for the Applied Innovation Exchange a few years earlier, Joe noted that the audience photo featured the traditional Capgemini demographic. "It looked like a Brioni advertisement. All these beautiful suits and high-end fabrics, very elegant." Fast forward to today, with the Idean team sharing the first floor, right when you walk in. "We have our first office dog. And it's common to see hip jeans and tshirts," said Joe adding somewhat incredulously. "The first person I ever saw in a company meeting wearing shorts was Risto."

To Joe, Risto brought the giant Capgemini a unique energy, "Loud and fun, aggressive and creative, inviting and international." Having immersed himself in a study of corporate management, Joe was more and more convinced that "a company could only go as far as the mindset of its leaders. "Risto is a guy who made the overt choice to build a name and get to know people in a place he's not from, by having awesome parties. That's Risto: 'How you do anything is how you do everything.'"

This shift Joe spoke about opened Risto to an incredible range of clients globally and in the US. Soon, Idean was working closely with industry leaders like Airbus, Apple, Mercedes, Amazon, GoPro, Samsung, Pfizer, and 23andMe. Risto could now truly pursue his vision, pushing the boundaries and possibilities of design in our increasingly digital world. He got down to business and quickly spotted and brought in a talented 30-person Capgemini group from Norway, and then acquired a team of 50 with the design agency Adaptive Lab in London. By mid 2018, in less than a year, his tiny Helsinki firm had doubled from 150 to 300. By the close of 2019, as he brought in other skilled Capgemini designers, Idean was knocking on 700 employees, with more than 23 studios in Europe, the US and Asia Pacific. Fresh from the success of his major IBM design transformation work, Risto was exploring new versions of design language and design thinking, holding his first event in the spring of 2019 on a new approach he calls "creating signature moments" for clients, underlining the moment in a customer journey that "surprises and delights."

This was about building a movement, his Next Big Thing. He had no written plan for the future, and if you asked him, he would smile and not answer. Ever since he'd been a boy he'd believed that, "If I go and tell my next dream to anyone too early it vanishes, it disappears."

Risto's story...isn't finished.

The Conductor
Carlos's Trial by Fire

Carlos's next fabulous project, located in the heart of SF's new tech hub, would be colossal. "The Transbay Terminal is enormous, a million square feet including a rooftop park and a 'box' of a basement that'll someday...accommodate trains including California's perpetually-in-development high-speed rail system," wrote *Wired*. "Enrobed in an undulating white metal mesh, the building cuts east-west like a cyborg kaiju eel swimming among downtown skyscrapers, bridging two busy boulevards." Yet this seventh wonder of the San Francisco Bay Area lacked one critical element. "They were going to open this multibillion-dollar terminal, and there had been thousands of people going through every day, but they didn't have any service," said Carlos. "No restaurants, no cafés, no nothing for many years. So they asked me: "Could you do food trucks and beer gardens and activate the space?"

Carlos's third major food truck park would prove capricious. Six months of planning, countless public meetings, followed by excruciating construction delays. The terminal finally opened in August of 2018, and Carlos's trucks were doing a bustling business until one fateful day in September when a maintenance worker stumbled upon a foot and a half crack running through a girder holding up the colossal roof. After just six weeks, the Transbay terminal abruptly closed, in turn shuttering Carlos's new food truck park. Experts were brought in and it took months to fix. With all the mistakes there was a changing of the guards. Recalled Carlos: "Everyone got fired, there were lawsuits, it was a crazy mess. And so when it all picked up again, I lost that deal." After his successes at SoMa and Spark, this came as a shock. The contract was awarded to Off the Grid. "It hurt because my competitor took it over," said Carlos, who had yet to experience failure. "It was kind of like a low blow."

Then came another blow, a second trial of his character. The following June of 2019 Carlos was working at his office when he heard a fire had broken out at Spark. He ran toward the blaze. "You see a huge plume of smoke. I'm thinking the whole place blew up, and people died." Photos would later show smoke rising several hundred feet above the city. What began as a small electrical spark in a small shed rapidly spread to Spark's adjoining AstroTurf field and burst into flames.

Fortunately no one was hurt, but the damage had been done. A grim-faced fire marshal paid a visit the next day, and Spark was shut down for weeks in the middle of the highly profitable summer season. To Carlos this was a huge gut check. He suddenly realized his enormous responsibility to the community to create a safe gathering place, and the consequences were immediate and severe. "The agencies tightened everything up. Whether it's assembly permits, egresses, exits, health department staff, you name it. Everybody came down on me."

Just when Carlos might truly scale and expand to a higher level he was being tested in ways he'd never anticipated. "There were waves of closures and openings," he recalled. "Weeks on end. Stressful times. A lot of hearings." But there was a difference now. Carlos had a substantial company with roughly 50 full and part time employees. Their support through this trying time meant the world to him, and by the fall of 2019 the clouds began to clear. He survived the intense city scrutiny, and his two original parks were thriving. He won a deal for another food truck park nearby on second street, and then in the bustling mid-Market area. The nearby town of Pacifica had also reached out. It was hard to believe, but Carlos had been doing this for nearly a decade straight out of college. He'd suffered two big setbacks in a year, but had the courage and resolve to ride out it. Now he was smarter and more sophisticated than ever before. He'd pioneered a system and platform the world wanted.

He was just 32. Who could tell what he'd create next?

The Guardian
Karoli Weighs the Numbers

The entrepreneur's dilemma unfolding right before Karoli Hindriks's eyes could be summed up in this potent question: "Do you listen to your gut, or the data?" Karoli had gone far on passion and intuition. She had traveled to the other side of the world and back, from tiny Tallinn, Estonia. All on a hunch, chasing the dream of a startup, powered by her passion for a cause, her stubborn belief that by sheer dint of imagination and drive, she – Karoli Hindriks – could bring to life this worldwide mobile workforce revolution called Jobbatical.

By the fall of 2018, the ground was shifting. When the Estonian government invited Jobbatical to apply for the national bidding process for immigration, Karoli thought, *This must be some sort of mistake.* Jobbatical's business was international job recruitment. And by many measures they'd succeeded, signing up users from every country in the world. But the government had also heard how Jobbatical excelled at the tricky supporting task of arranging for visas and work permits, a skill that clicked with Estonia's desperate need for more IT talent. Jobbatical made a bid, won it, and that was just the start.

"It made perfect sense for Jobbatical to dig deeper into this," Karoli would later say. "Because immigration is the monster under the bed of global hiring." By February of 2019, Karoli recognized that her side business delivering the nuts and bolts of immigration was threatening to become her main business. Fast-growing tech firms like Twilio, Veriff, Pipedrive and TransferWise counted on her for international growth. In comparison, Jobbatical's recruiting platform was struggling.

"By May I had a very clear understanding that the numbers were talking," said Karoli. The immigration business had boomed to 40 percent of their total revenue, expanding by a phenomenal 20 percent a month. "However much I loved my original idea of Jobbatical, it was no longer a gut feeling, the numbers were just there."

Karoli was staring down a pivotal decision. On one hand there was her original dream. On the other, a fresh opportunity to scale, discovered in the true push and shove of serving global customers. "My fear was that I now had to convince my team," she recalled. "How will I do that?" By June of 2019, Karoli was already dramatically shifting resources. Her team could gain approvals for most European visas in a scant two weeks. In Estonia, they could land a work permit in an astonishing 4-8 hours.

Smack in the middle of the glorious Baltic summer Karoli dismissed half her young company – slimming down to under 25 employees, because, as she put it: "we just didn't need recruiting anymore." It was a painful decision because many of these individuals had been so dedicated to Jobbatical's original mission. With the downsizing, Karoli accelerated the automation of immigration to create a kind of TurboTax for immigration. The goal: a seamless process requiring little to no individual involvement with the local government, "so that a company doesn't have to worry about how immigration works – you can just continue hiring." Veriff, an anti-identify fraud startup in Estonia, was one of her best success stories, having relied on Jobbatical to grow its headcount an astonishing 17-fold in one year, from 18 to 300 – in 40 different countries.

Scale. Expansion. Acceleration. Karoli was delivering the technology platform needed for the human side of growth. By summer's end, Karoli had deployed dedicated teams in the hot markets of Germany, the Czech Republic, and Spain. Her website became streamlined, with a Stanford Launchpad-style targeted offering: "Hire whoever you want – we'll relocate them for you. We take care of the entire talent immigration and relocation process for you, saving you time and providing a delightful experience for your new employees." She planned to open three or four offices each subsequent quarter, and could already envision a new capability. "The more we expand, the more we'll be able to identify very specific country-by-country global mobility trends." Valuable data, in other words, since scaling human talent is a critical barometer of a city or region's economic growth.

This was a different Jobbatical, with the potential to achieve a similar goal at far greater scale. "The companies we are working with have told us that they are more confident about hiring from abroad," said Karoli. "And the more we reduce their fear, the more openness and diversity are being built." The next phase is technological immigration integration within entire countries, starting with Malaysia and Estonia. "So imagine if Jobbatical has integrations with all these different governments and immigration becomes so easy that you don't even have to interface with the government besides providing a fingerprint," Karoli explained, with the same visionary enthusiasm as when she first dreamed up the platform, nearly six years earlier at Singularity University.

Her mission hadn't changed. She was still firmly targeting the inequality that had rocked her on that morning jog by Google. "Still building bridges between talent and employers to distribute brilliant ideas and minds more evenly around the planet. And now we know that by solving immigration, we can bring about change on a bigger scale."

The Guardian, in the push and shove of building her own start-up, had discovered where she could tip the balance of power away from Silicon Valley to the rest of the world.

Takeaways:
Scaling Up

Growth. Expansion. The critical point at which the gears start turning. The mountaintop is within range, the goal you've been shooting for now within sight. What Faces do you need to Scale?

Makers build a community of makers.
Evangelists broadcast their next big thing.
Accidentals own their new expertise.
Conductors vary the model — big, small or in between.
Visionaries have a great sense of timing.
Athletes focus on the fundamentals: body, mind, performance.
Collaborators take the next step of growth: They become leaders.
Guardians make the leap by listening to the mission.
Leaders focus on their tribe and the next generation.
Outsiders exit and open a new door.

EPILOGUE: THE FUTURE

S cale is the final stage in our book, but it's by no means a last chapter for an entrepreneur. On the contrary, scale is a hopeful rite of passage. The realization of a goal that provides a fresh vision for the future. Having proven your venture has legs, now is the time for a different kind of growth — whether linear, lateral, or exponential.

You've likely picked up on something that may not have been clear when you started reading this book. We have told our characters' stories through the lens of their dominant archetype, the Face that most prominently represents their mindset and nature. But we are not locked into any one persona. People adapt and change. We wake up one day and want to be more of an Athlete or Collaborator. Or find ourselves hungry to take on an Outsider mindset to discover less obvious opportunities. Instead of dwelling on perceived limitations, or getting stuck in the past, we can split off from what would seem to be our planned trajectory, and glimpse ahead, peer around the curve to someone we hope to be.

Yes, Uwe was a consummate Evangelist, but also a prolific Maker. Mait, our Accidental, stumbled into his role as a startup founder yet he is also now growing into a Visionary, carving a path toward a radical new approach to learning. Karoli is as committed a Guardian as you will find on the planet, but she and her company wouldn't still be standing if she wasn't a terrific Athlete. She dashed barefoot through the streets of Helsinki to make a crucial investor meeting and then five years later, had the courage and strength to totally pivot her focus to streamlining immigration for fast-growing companies. This ability to shape-shift makes entrepreneurs light on their feet, providing flexibility and speed at key junctures. The Faces give a form to who we are becoming, and as you set out on your entrepreneurial journeys we hope they speak to you and help you become your best possible self.

Learning to identify the entrepreneurial types is another way of maximizing your potential. Who do you need on your team as you Launch or go for the Money? When you're battered by the series of tribulations we call the Test and need to try something you've never done before, consider which type you might surface to help navigate to success.

As we write these words in June of 2020 we are facing an unprecedented public health threat and economic crisis. We don't believe the ultimate solution will be isolation. Pain often spurs the entrepreneurially minded to experiment. The global pandemic is a huge Test for us all – including, not surprisingly, the ten extraordinary people you've gotten to know in these pages. They're facing the crisis with courage, resilience, and yes, creativity. Taking bold, new steps is never easy.

We consider ourselves fortunate to be collaborating with some thought leaders in the world of UX design, video conferencing, and online learning. We're experimenting with how entrepreneurs and intrapreneurs can come together over the Internet to share and build upon good ideas, and develop new products. Now, more than ever, is a time for an Awakening toward a new way of working. We have already made our initial Shift.

We invite you to join us.

ACKNOWLEDGMENTS

Here in San Francisco we've watched tech waves come and go: the personal computer revolution, the dawn of the Internet and Web, the dotcom boom and bust, and the sharing economy. We noticed something different in 2012. The global entrepreneurial startup craze was catching fire. Incubators and co-working places began opening at a frantic clip in the city, and we found ourselves drawn to tech events, pitch nights, and panels featuring American authors and big tech thought leaders. San Francisco was becoming what we call a Place, and we began meeting extraordinary people who had a huge role in changing our thinking about entrepreneurship. Allan Young, whom you know from the book, was instrumental. His bustling accelerator, boasting an igloo, and eighty startups, was located in the Twitter building. Runway seemed to represent a microcosm of what was happening throughout the city and around the world.

We learned about entrepreneurship by meeting and interviewing hundreds of entrepreneurs. Anne Cocquyt, the indefatigable founder of the women's networking platform The GUILD, became a key mentor in our entrepreneurship class at the University of San Francisco, a great model for how talented young people are boldly fashioning less traditional careers. Because we ultimately opted for a narrative with a limited number of characters (first a dozen, then trimmed down to ten), most of the people we met over the next several years did not wind up our book, but we haven't forgotten their contributions. Carlos Oliveira and Torben Rankine of Leadership Business Consulting of Lisbon began hiring Jon in 2012 to give talks in San Francisco and later in Portugal for groups from Portugal, Brazil, Mozambique and Angola, affording him an early taste of the international hunger for entrepreneurship and innovation. Jon also is grateful to University of San Francisco Professor Mark Cannice, Jenny Fogarty, Cynthia Bi, and Professor Rebecca Tower who gave him many opportunities to teach his favorite class, Creativity, Innovation and Applied Design and year after year brought him amazing cohorts of MBAs and executives from all over Europe and China for his immersive innovation labs.

By early 2015, Susanna became editor-in-chief of SmartUp.life, turning what was first a casual blog, into a serious chronicle of entrepreneurship and innovation, a place to write about this revolution. Susanna has long had a nose for trends. She joined *Wired*, the hot, iconic magazine just after its launch and rose to become a team leader. More recently in the last several years, as the vibrant tech event scene in San Francisco heated up, she knew she had to play a bigger role in the evolving ecosystem. Skipping work at her day job to attend conferences led by NewCo and BootstrapLabs, became her new, healthy habit. She started meeting startup founders and chronicling their stories, and soon took a second position as Editorial Director of The GUILD, eventually going independent with her skills in writing, social media, and tech.

Our collective international focus – working with students and executives from nearly 20 countries – led us to our own lightbulb Awakening in 2017. We saw all around us that attitude and mindset were as critical to personal success as technology and investment. One night that spring, we signed up for a different kind of experience, at the Runway accelerator. This wasn't the usual mélange of entrepreneurs, coders and startups. The chatter was in several languages. Guest badges displayed a foreign bent: government officials, trade bureau representatives, and businesspeople assembled to hear the findings of a promising major report about an international upswell. We learned of the new wave of enthusiasm for tech entrepreneurism in Europe, epitomized by Paris's 1,000-strong new startup colossus Station F, the election of French President Macron, and the rise of impressive European tech hubs in London, Berlin, Amsterdam, Stockholm, Lisbon, and a host of other cities. This wasn't just Silicon Valley or San Francisco. There was a far wider, more diverse world of feverish innovation and entrepreneurism emerging beyond the Bay Area, and we wanted to go see it, feel it, chronicle it. We set off on our own extended road trip, and over the next fourteen months, spent nearly five months traveling through Europe, documenting our findings for SmartUp.life, visiting countless incubators and attending numerous international conferences. And as we met and profiled scores of fascinating innovators, we grasped a common structure in the shape of their backstories that ultimately became the framework of the book.

Special thanks go to six individuals who, because our narrative structure changed midstream, did not make the final pages. Tomas Moreno, Head of Culture Transformation at Energias de Portugal, generously granted us multiple interviews, as did the impressive young futurist Alida Draudt. Mathieu Guerville, a talented innovation director and startup veteran, provided us great insights into the entrepreneurial mindset. There was Ayleen Nazario, who beat the odds and interned her way to her dream job at Google, part of a new generation of youths who are incredibly entrepreneurial in how they build up their profile in high school and college. We only met Stefan Batory of Booksy once in Warsaw but we loved his story, and he also nearly made the book (he had the discipline to eat only potatoes for two years to save money). Kevin Smith of The Vault, a great international incubator in San Francisco that we wrote about frequently in SmartUp because of its excellent events, graciously sat for an extended interview.

Thanks to Nilson Kufus of Nomoko, a swissnex incubee, we met Andreas Schollin-Borg of Gotham and Batmaid, Key Portilla Kawamura of Studio Banana, and Tej Tadi of MindMaze in Switzerland during our first European foray. In Paris, thanks to our friendship with Warsaw-based Kinga Stanislawska, who knew Station F director Roxanne Varza, we met Antoine Leprêtre, director of the HEC incubator and Guillaume le Dieu de Ville, of HEC-42 Startup Launchpad, Emanuel Allely of Usine, and Jonathan Chester of Bitwage. Our connection to Capgemini led us to Deputy Mayor of Credit Agricole's Le Village, Benoît Bourdin. We are also grateful to Catherine Madinier and Anthony Civitas of the innovative international coding school 42. In Lisbon we met Siim Sikkut, Estonia's Princeton-educated Chief Innovation Officer, who introduced us to nearly twenty people in Tallinn, two of whom, Karoli Hindriks and Mait Müntel, wound up in our book. As we headed north, we were tremendously impressed by the Heart incubator in Warsaw and Pawel Michalski, Tomasz Rudolf and Barbara Sobowska proved generous hosts as was Rune Thiell of the Amsterdam incubator Rockstart. Ruben Nieuwenhuis, co-director of StartUpAmsterdam, not only invited us to speak at his Startup City Summit but introduced us to Hans Meyer, creative founder of one of the coolest hotels/co-working hubs in town, if not the world, Zoku. Nina Ehrsam, Patrick Consorti, and Eric Thelen of EIT Digital connected us to Risto Lähdesmäki, which led us to crash his party at a Michelin-starred bistro in Helsinki during the intense Slush conference, and ultimately include him in the book. Special thanks to Bob Sutton, the bestselling author and Stanford professor who introduced us to Perry Klebahn of Stanford Launchpad. Both Perry and fellow Launchpad lead, Jeremy Utley, generously invited Jon to attend many sessions over the course of two years, and introduced him to a number of talented alumni, including Ben Knelman of Juntos, Jon Beekman of Man Crates, and of course, Daniel Lewis, profiled in the book.

Place is one of our central concepts in *The Entrepreneur's Faces*, and we couldn't have written it without practicing what we preach. While presenting an early version of SmartUp to a crowd at the University of San Francisco, Jon first met the food truck king Carlos Muela. While researching a SmartUp story about the thriving Santa Barbara ecosystem, and visiting colleagues Max James and Kyle Ashby, we met Joel Heath and rode his Level balance board. Capgemini's Applied Innovation Center in San Francisco played a key role. Susanna's former colleague at Wired, Pete Leyden produces the impressive series What's Now SF, and it was there that we met Joe Boggio.

Where in the world did we find a character like Uwe Diegel?

During our first Web Summit in Lisbon, we spotted him pitching in the contest, just one of a thousand contestants, and pulled him aside for a quick interview. It was only later we learned that a couple of days later in front of a live audience of 12,000 he had taken the grand prize.

We are deeply grateful to the many talented international entrepreneurs we met on our journey, and would like to thank them here:

Max Kelly of TechStars, Kinga Jentetics of PublishDrive, Henry Wang of NIO, Zenel Batagelj of Cofound.it, Tim Zagar, co-founder of Iconomi, and his lawyer Nejc Novak, Slovenian trade minister Tadej Slapnik, Nena Dukozov, the head of the Cultural Centre of European Space Technologies, Petri Martikainen of Moprim, Roemer Claasen of Frosha, Igor Ponikarchik and Vlad Herchykau of Bamboo Group, Teymour Khalatbari and Juliette Dusseaux of Dalia, Peter Mayer of Der Flipper, PlateWithMate founder Zuzanna Grudniak, Evgeniy Ursalov, Andrey Konoplenko, and Rodion Salnik, the young founders of Casers, Herminio Garcia of Budsy, Kevin Perlmutter, Limbic Brand Evolution, Raphaël Bord and Jonathan Cottrel of Credit Agricole, Startup Amsterdam's Bas Beekman and Ruben Nieuwenhuis, Zoku's Marc Jongerius, Hans Meyer, and Identity and Design Manager Veerle Donders, Bram de Zwart of 3D Hubs, Elad Kobi and Eyal Moshe in Tel Aviv, Indrek Onnik of e-Estonia Showroom, Ragnar Sass of Lift99 and Pipedrive, Valeo's Federico Pardo Saguier and Philippine Heron Auge, Olga Barreto Gonçalves of the Investment and Development Agency of Latvia, Karen Bhatia of the NYC Economic Development Corporation, Jarmo Lauronen of BusinessOulu, Eduarda Pinto, Executive Director of Lionesa, André Forte and Joao Afonso of Startup Portugal, Daniela Monteiro of Porto Digital, Alexandre Santos of Bright Pixel, Ricardo Marvão, co-founder of Beta-i, Ricardo Lopes of Fivehundred, José Mota Leal and Sandra Pereira of Hub Criativo, Alexander Helmer, co-founder of Jungle, Gianluca Pereyra, co-founder of Visor.ai, author Amiel Kornel, Pedro and João Presa of Mycujoo, Matthieu Lecuyer, the co-founder and CMO of R-PUR, and Nick Yap of Zoi Meet.

They say it takes a village, and we found our village in the countless talented students, entrepreneurs and executives we met while delivering workshops and leading classes these past several years. We discovered validation in their enthusiasm, and couldn't have finished the book without their support.